THE SPARROW GARDEN

Peter Skrzynecki was born in 1945 in Germany and came to Australia in 1949. He has published fifteen books of poetry and prose. His work has been translated into several languages including Greek, Polish, Turkish, Spanish, Vietnamese, Ukrainian and German. His prizes include the Captain Cook Bi-Centennial Award, the Grace Leven Poetry Prize and the Henry Lawson Short Story Award. In 1989 he received the Order of Cultural Merit from the Polish Government and in 2002 the Medal of the Order of Australia (OAM) for services to Australian multicultural literature, particularly as a poet. He is an associate professor in the School of Humanities at the University of Western Sydney.

By the same author

Immigrant Chronicle
Joseph's Coat: An Anthology of Multicultural Writing (editor)
The Wild Dogs (short stories)
The Beloved Mountain (novel)
Night Swim (poetry)
Rock'n'Roll Heroes (short stories)
Easter Sunday (poetry)
The Cry of the Goldfinch (novel)
Influence: Australian Voices (editor)
Time's Revenge (poetry)

THE SPARROW GARDEN

Peter Skrzynecki

UQP

Published 2004 by University of Queensland Press
Box 6042, St Lucia, Queensland 4067 Australia

Reprinted 2008

www.uqp.uq.edu.au

Printed in Australia by McPherson's Printing Group

Sponsored by the Queensland Office
of Arts and Cultural Development.

Cataloguing in Publication Data
National Library of Australia

Skrzynecki, Peter, 1945– .
  The sparrow garden.

  1. Skrzynecki, Peter, 1945– — Childhood and youth. 2.
  Poets, Australian — 20th century — Biography. 3.
  Immigrants — Australia — Biography. I. Title.

A821.3

ISBN 978 0 7022 3426 2

For my parents
Kornelia Woloszczuk (9.11.1917–6.2.1997)
&
Feliks Skrzynecki (16.2.1905–26.6.1994)

"Moja Służba"

"Perhaps the mysteries of transformation and the enigmas of life which so torment us are concentrated in the green of the earth, among the trees in graveyards and the flowering shoots springing from their beds. Mary Magdalene, not at once recognising Jesus risen from the grave, took Him for the gardener."

Boris Pasternak, *Doctor Zhivago*

Contents

Part I
The Sparrow Garden   *3*
Anzac Day   *12*
Snow Is Falling   *26*
Water   *32*
The Day that Lasted Forever   *39*
Strays   *49*
The Sewage Works   *58*
The Circular Saw Accident   *66*
10 Mary Street   *82*
Eels   *93*
The Holiday Outing   *103*
Good Morning, Sister, God Bless You   *117*
Cracker Night   *144*
Two Boys Fighting   *154*
Last Performance   *162*

Part II
Bullseye!   *171*
Failings   *188*
Next Stop for Me, Doctor ...   *199*
Closed Venetian Blinds   *219*
Sprzedaj!   *225*

Acknowledgments

A first draft of "The Day that Lasted Forever" first appeared in *Country Childhoods*, ed. Geoffrey Dutton, University of Queensland Press, St Lucia, 1992.

Trials to Triumph 1937–1987: A History of St Peter Chanel, Berala, The First 50 Years, Parish of Berala, 1987.

The Book of Sydney Suburbs, compiled by Frances Pollon, Angus & Robertson, Sydney, 1988.

Time's Revenge, Brandl & Schlesinger, Sydney, 2000, for "Sayings" and "Billycart Days".

Five Bells, Volume 7, No. 4, October 2000 (Poets Union Inc.) for "Only Child".

No River Is Safe (Poets Union Inc. Anthology 2000), ed. Margaret Bradstock, 2001, for "Sunday Visits".

Quadrant, May, 2003 for "Roses".

All other poems are from *Immigrant Chronicle*, University of Queensland Press, St Lucia. First published 1975. Reprinted 1992, 1993, 1994, 2002, 2003.

Special thanks to my wife, Kate, and my children, Judy, Andrew and Anna, for their patience and support during the writing of this memoir. Also, those friends who shared their memories and provided information: the Tom brothers, of Parkes, and their wives; Maria Dziuba and her mother, Helena, also of Parkes; Irene Salinger, Al Zolynas, Andy Milcz, Kevin Coates and Rev. Brother Brian Berg; Catherine Panich; Marianna Lacek; Dr John Hehir; Tony Garnett and Charles

Burford. For their encouragement, Ivor Indyk and Geoffrey Cains. Also, for their encouragement and editorial advice, Madonna Duffy and Craig Munro at University of Queensland Press. Last but by no means least, that indomitable source of laughter and commonsense, my literary agent, Barbara Mobbs, for all the above reasons and more.

I

The Sparrow Garden

For as long as I can remember there were sparrows in the garden, from when we moved into 10 Mary Street, Regents Park in 1951, until now, forty-six years later, when both parents have died and I've come over to the house, to air it, clear out the junk mail and water the garden ... There they are, flitting about the lawns and gardens — energetic, restless, industriously searching for food, twittering among themselves and keeping me company, just like they did when I was a boy, filling the silence of the backyard.

My mother died three weeks ago, less two days, though at times it seems like yesterday, and at other times like the proverbial eternity.

One of the images I have is of her feeding the sparrows, standing on the back steps of the house, throwing crusts or crumbs to them, scraps of food, while they hop across the lawn towards her, pecking, looking up, pecking, pecking, then flying off, only to return for the next handful she throws out.

Family, friends, people of charitable intent tell me that I am passing through the first phase of grief, that I am still numbed and the tears will come spontaneously, whether I want them to or not.

And so they do, as I water the garden and stand still with sunlight warming my face, with water running from the hose on to my hand because the nozzle leaks.

The garden is smelling fresh, of vegetation, of water and soil, like it does after rain.

A week before my mother died an incident occurred here, almost where I am standing, that still has a disturbing effect on me.

I arrived one morning to drop off some shopping.

To go to work for the past twelve years I've had to pass through Regents Park. So, where my parents were concerned, it was no great effort to stop off and help them, bring in shopping, do the fortnightly banking, take them to the hairdresser when necessary, help with house cleaning and assist in whatever way I could. That particular morning my mother was cheerful and bright. There was a lightness in her voice that belied the effects of her "desh asthma", as she called it, and the bad night she'd experienced. She was a severe asthmatic, and in the last few years of her life had to be on a ventilator every four or five hours.

When I arrived she'd just finished using the machine, but you could still make out the wheezing that came from her chest when she spoke.

We were in the kitchen. Look what's in my garden.

She was smiling. She stood at the sink and pointed proudly out the window to the patch of garden, between the kitchen and the outside toilet, where two large camellias grew surrounded by salvias and balsams.

I can't see anything.

Huh, that's because you still haven't learnt how to use your eyes properly.

I followed the line of her finger but could see only flowers.

No, sorry.

Come with me. She gave a little smile as if to say, "You think I'm old and silly." She crooked her index finger for me to follow, winking as she did.

Outside it was cooler than in the house because this back

section of the garden was in shadow, but there was sunlight where we stood.

See, they've been here every morning this week.

As if on cue, soft, short trumpet calls sounded at our feet. I looked down and saw the cause of her delight.

Two zebra finches, a normal chestnut male and a white female were hopping around in the garden bed, oblivious to our presence, feeding on grasses and some fibrous matter they'd discovered among the flowers.

See, she repeated, they've been visiting me. It must be a sign from your father.

It means they've escaped from someone's aviary and have found breakfast in your garden.

Disturbed by our rising voices the birds flew off, perched on the paling fence and watched us, continuing to send their stabbing notes into the morning air.

I grew up in that house, spent the post–World War II decades watching a suburb of bushland turned gradually into factories, industrial workshops, houses. I learnt the name of every bird that lived in the area. Bird names were as familiar to me as my own — sparrow, willy-wagtail, blue wren, swallow, peewit, magpie, the blue cranes that flew over Duck Creek. In the early days there were even kingfishers. As a boy I received a small whitewashed aviary with two zebra finches one year as a birthday present from Charley White, the boarder who lived across the road at Mrs Cutler's. I thought I knew everything there was to know about zebra finches … but never had I seen them flying free in our backyard.

As I stared at the birds, my mother said, That's me and your father. We'll come back and visit you after I've gone.

With those words, the female flew back to our feet, or rather to my mother's feet, and called plaintively to her mate who promptly flew back. They cocked their heads to look up at the old woman who was now holding out her hands to them.

I was nonexistent.

Time stopped.

My mother made a rapid waving motion with her hands and the birds flew off, over the back fence and into the reserve, their piping calls becoming small darts, hitting me with their needle points.

The spell was broken.

Your father might be dead, my mother smiled, but he still listens to me and comes when I call him. Looking me in the eyes, she added, Don't be sad. We'll always be here in spirit. All three of us.

I have to be going, Mum, or I'll be late for work.

She saw me off to the front gate as she always did and waited until I drove away, waving as I turned the car around and headed off, waving back, glancing over my shoulder.

I saw an old woman in house clothes, attire she'd made herself, a scarf wrapped around her head and shoulders, an old woman who was my mother, stooped and leaning on the top railing of a blue-and-white gate, the paling fence behind her overgrown with star jasmine. She was partly hidden by roses and gardenias, brunfelsias that fronted the road, behind a fence that enclosed a red brick-veneer house that was once my home, in front of a garden that had been filled with flowers taller than myself, so many flowers I could not remember their names. The garden that my parents called Paradise.

The hose is heavy as I drag it further down the yard, towards the two remaining fruit trees, a mandarin and a lemon, growing in front of the toilet and chookshed.

Sparrows scatter as I advance.

Once there were stone fruits as well, blood plums and nectarines that my mother would bottle and preserve. All that is left of that practice today are the empty preserving jars and lids stored in one of the cupboards in the laundry.

The soil at the base of the trees soaks up the water thirstily and I let it run until it overflows the circular brick edges that my father built around the trees. Part of his gardening activities included keeping these bases free of weeds and the soil turned, fresh and fertilised with blood and bone. When dead branches, scale or borers appeared he would promptly prune the trees and spray them, or he would dig out the borers with the end of a straightened wire coathanger, my mother helping him by holding the branch — both parents on ladders or chairs, assisting each other, working together.

To my right, the old fibro chookshed's corrugated-iron roof catches my eye and I'm drawn to the corner where a few strands of grass stick out. I know there is a sparrow's nest under there, in that exact spot, just as there has been for years. I know that by lifting the corner of the roof, I can put in my hand and probably find what I found once, as a boy — a clutch of five or six eggs, greyish white, speckled with peppery-brown spots. From then on, each summer or spring, when I knew the sparrows were breeding, I would climb on top of the dog kennel directly below the roof and lift up the corner, even though it meant forcing the metal sheet upwards. Sure enough, there would be a nest made of grasses and lined with feathers, pieces of wool or string, a nest that contained eggs or tiny wide-beaked baby birds with large protruding eyes, closed, opening their yellow beaks because they thought it was a parent returning with food. The nest always had a peculiar smell that was a combination of bird dust and droppings and dried grasses, an odour of another world that I would learn, when I grew up, was caused by bird lice.

My head turns in the opposite direction, towards the other side of the garden where vegetables used to be grown.

All that is left are small clumps of chives and onions, their stalks bent and dried, withering. Similar to what's left of the potatoes, cucumbers, beetroots, tomatoes, corn, carrots. Weeds grow among them, their small white flowers shining like cut glass above the yellow-and-green stalks.

The weeds benefit the most when I water the garden, because they have almost taken over the patch. After my father's death my mother spent less time in the garden, though initially there was an intention to keep everything "as it used to be". As her health deteriorated, less time was spent tending the vegetables as she concentrated on caring for her beloved roses and camellias.

But memory can play tricks; it can take unexpected twists and change a pleasant image into one of violence.

My eyes become rivetted to a spot where lettuce was grown and I hear *thud thud thud* in rapid succession as a piece of wood is brought down on wire netting that covers small heads of lettuce. Beneath the wire, small bodies are trapped; they flutter and try to escape. Again, *thud thud*. The wood my father uses as a club is an old sawn-off hoe handle. The birds are sparrows and they flutter frantically, madly. They twitter in fear and are in a live-or-die panic. But there will be no escape. My father is calling out "Husha!" "Husha!" to frighten away the birds. Of course it is too late.

This has happened before.

To protect their garden from the sparrows my parents have devised a system of wire covers for the different vegetables they grow from seedlings. Should there be sparrows that have found their way under the covers — and there were those that always did — when one or either of my parents came outside, it was easy to get to the club that was kept within the garden's perimeter. At first I used to protest, try to warn the birds, but my parents quickly asserted authority over their garden and literally pushed me into the background. Later, the little corpses were chucked over the back fence into the bush or taken down and dumped into Duck Creek.

The sparrows were never eradicated totally, and, along with various kinds of scarecrows that my father created out of old shirts and hats hung on crosses, this method of disposal remained for a long time. But at some point in our lives in Mary Street it changed, and although the wire coverings stayed, the clubbing became less frequent, until it stopped altogether. Maybe my parents relented, gave in to a realisation that the sparrows were here to stay. So it became enough to frighten them off at our approach, and although there were holes left in the lettuce leaves, the sparrows escaped. Secretly, I was pleased.

The time for my visit is drawing to an end and I finish watering the garden.

I still have to complete a few small jobs, but know from past practice that within ten minutes I will be on my way.

Turning off the hose at the tap under the kitchen window, I disconnect it and attempt to coil it, lasso-style, like my father used to. Water runs out both ends, on to my shoes and trousers, over my hands and shirtsleeves. It's a skill I have never perfected and probably never will.

With the hose coiled the best way I can, I half carry, half drag it into the chookshed and see the water trail left behind me along the footpath, snaking its way like a dribble of thoughts, half lost, broken and incomplete, trying to catch up and attract my attention. Water should never be wasted: that was one of the cardinal rules I was raised on. Nor should electricity, or food, or the hundred-and-one components that make up our daily existence. I don't know who is responsible for the saying "Waste not, want not", but if I didn't know better I would say it was one of my parents or someone from that European generation who emigrated to Australia after the Second World War. They were people who survived on their instincts for a long time and learned to value every morsel of food or drop of water that came into their lives. If I had done the job I was doing correctly, I would have wound the hose on the grass — and water would not have been wasted.

Now the house has to be closed again.

When I arrive here I first open the front door and windows, prop open the back door so that fresh air runs through it, from one side of the house to the other. When I open the window in my mother's bedroom, at the front of the house, I always stop to see how much the curtains will flutter. The more they flutter, the stronger the breeze blowing through the house. That's a good sign, I think. A sign of new breath, renewal.

The voice in my head says, "You're going away again", and a feeling like nothing else on earth comes over me, a heaviness, a laboured breathing, slow, as if each breath might be my last, the physical experience of the word *żal*. It sounds like the house is speaking to me. Even though I stopped crying back in the garden, even though I know I will return tomorrow or the next day to check on the house, on the garden, and talk to myself and my parents as if they were still alive. Even though I don't know what to do with the house at present, whether to keep it or sell it.

One of the things I have learnt in the short space of time since my mother's death is that an empty house has a scent about it, an odour, that is authentic and somehow timeless. It is a combination of the human and elemental, of people and food, of clothes and the materials that make up the house. While someone is living there, you do not really notice it, but once the house is empty, it cannot be escaped. It follows you from room to room, as if to say, *You are a part of this also*. Or conversely, *I'm part of you. You cannot, will not, ever be free of me.* When I step inside the house, move from room to room, the combined smells of cooking, wearing clothes, using hand creams, soaps, body scents, the very condition of human habitation sweeps over me like a caul, swamps me, and its presence simultaneously pierces my consciousness like a needle. The air in the house is neither musty nor stale, it belongs neither to yesterday nor tomorrow. It is the present, vibrant and real, as tangible as the door handles that I trail my fingers over, as real as the floral carpet under my feet or the ice forming in the refrigerator that I keep telling myself I must turn off the next time I am here.

I check that the timers are on, that they will come on in one of the bedrooms and the dining room at six o'clock, switch on and off at various intervals until eleven o'clock. With the door between the kitchen and dining room left open, the light will also shine into the kitchen. That way, there will be a light in both the back and front of the house.

Having secured the house, double-checking that the back door is locked, I leave it to the late afternoon sun, to the birds that live on the land, and to the ghosts of my parents, the pet dogs and cats we had, the ducks and chooks we bred, the birds I kept, all the visitors who trod its grounds, who marvelled at its fecundity, wished us well in our new home in Australia, the home that would be ours from 1951 to 1997. Once I am gone the sparrows will return, searching among the weeds for places where water has collected in pools.

As my car turns out of Mary Street I push the gear selector into Drive and press my foot on to the accelerator at the same time, hard. There is a surge of power from the V6 engine and the Commodore rushes along Clapham Road.

How can I forget what happened in the house three weeks less two days ago?

25 February 1997

Anzac Day

25 April 1997

Today, Judy and I meet at 10 Mary Street to give the place a good cleaning and mow the lawns. We have arranged this beforehand. We figured, it being Anzac Day, there would be little traffic on the roads and we could work at our leisure, without it mattering what time we finished.

When I arrive at half-past nine she is already there, mopping the veranda as she used to do when Mum was alive, turning the dusty tiles into a mirror of red and orange glazes. Mum's transistor plays from the sideboard; it is the ABC, with Richard Glover, and the program is about the history of Sydney's suburbs.

Exactly two weeks after my mother died I had my first dream of her. She was getting on the train at Strathfield station, on Platform 8, as we both used to do — she, returning home from one of her places of employment — me, returning from school at St Patrick's College. She was wearing her brown corduroy dress and carried a shopping bag over her arm. When she died she was seventy-nine, yet in this dream she was considerably younger, probably in her forties. Neither of us spoke but she appeared content, her features almost perfect, without blemish. In the months ahead, whenever I dream about her, alone or with my father, she will look like this, very much younger, and nearly always she — or they — will be travelling, moving on to somewhere.

Hi, Dad, Judy greets me.

Hello, daughter, I reply.

The formality of my greeting belies the love, the strength, the closeness that I feel for her, and I will never be able to explain to the world what a tower of strength this child has been to me since my mother died, especially those first twenty-four hours when I didn't sleep at all. Next day she drove me to Labor Funerals at Bankstown, to the Commonwealth Bank at Regents Park, to the stonemason at Lidcombe to arrange the lettering on the headstone, then back to 10 Mary Street, where we sat and talked, had some refreshments, tried to make sense out of the unexpectedness of death. My body needed sleep desperately; my eyes felt like they were on fire. I kept nodding off, but a voice in my brain would sound a warning, *No, no, you can't fall asleep!* All this time, it felt as if my mother was in the kitchen with us, giving us strength to cope with the funeral in four days' time.

I'll go around the back, I say, otherwise I'll leave marks on the veranda … You're doing a great job.

She says nothing and continues intently with her mopping, head down, as a hockey player might stand before striking for the ball.

The house has been opened up.

The front bedroom curtains flutter in the breeze.

I can smell the garden's freshness.

Sparrows fly up from the brunfelsias and roses, from where I know they have dust baths. The soil there has several small hollows, each one's diameter about the size of a tennis ball. The sparrows lie in these and dust themselves, especially when the sun is on the front garden, as it is now, because the house faces the east.

As I turn the corner and face the backyard a similar scent of freshness rises in the air.

The lawn that was once so spotless, so smooth and green that visitors used to congratulate my father and say, *You could*

play bowls on this, needs to be weeded and cut. Before entering
the house I go down to the chookshed, drag out the hose and
connect it to the tap. The immediate garden area next to the
house needs soaking.

The sparrows that flew off from the front have followed me
to the back. Or are they different ones? They perch on the gutters and fence, heads cocked, like the zebra finches did that
morning when I stopped in to see my mother. They might well
be asking, What are you humans doing here?

The laundry is open.

Under the louvre windows the old copper is empty, as are
the two concrete tubs. My mother's red peg bag hangs over the
edge of one and adds a brightness to an otherwise bland setting, even though the walls were originally painted an attrac-
tive pale blue. The peg bag resembles a piece of clothing and
seems out of place. She made it from a wooden coathanger by
sewing material over it, making a slit in the front and edging
that with green. I bump against the bag and the pegs rattle with
their unmistakable plastic sound. Black hoses run from the
washing machine over the sides of the tubs and up to the taps
like snakes. A pink baby blanket covers the top of the washing
machine. My mother did that for years, as a precautionary
measure, to protect the enamel.

On the other side of the laundry are the overhead and bench
cupboards; most of these are empty now but at one end they
contain a collection of shoes that my mother kept in boxes.
The cupboards also contain an assortment of jars, insecticides,
sprays, poisons, fertilisers that my parents used for the maintenance of the garden: Defender Snail Pellets, Malathon,
Baygon, Aquasol, blood and bone. Anything too big for these
cupboards was kept in the garage. On top of the benches were
the soaps ... Sunlight, Lux, Omo, Persil ... and even as I turn
around it's the smell of soaps, rather than insecticides, that fills
my nostrils, warm and soft. In one of the cupboards my parents kept the kerosene primus that was one of the "luxuries"

we brought from the migrant hostel in Parkes. The drawers are full of nails, screws, pencils, bits of string, coils of copper wire, tap washers, spanners, screwdrivers, old door handles, some studs from my football shoes, last worn in 1963, my last year at St Patrick's College. So much old stuff that I will spend weeks emptying it into the Otto bin. My mother's washing basket sits regally on top of the red lino bench; the cane is thick, strong, and has been woven tightly. Where it has broken or the weave come undone, it has been repaired. Beside it lies a piece of 2 × 2 timber, about a foot long: this is the door jamb that's used to prevent the door from swinging shut, as it does when a wind blows. The light cord has been the same since I can remember, like a long shoelace, worn smooth by three pairs of hands. The cement floor is a worn, faded green. When my father painted it we were warned to keep away until the paint had dried one hundred per cent. He took such pride in whatever he created manually, whether it was painting, digging a potato garden, building a fence or cementing a footpath. His son, on the other hand, can't hammer a nail without bending it.

A willy-wagtail dances in the lemon tree and tempts me outside with its "Sweet-pretty-creature" song. Somewhere, beyond the backyard fence, from the winding distance of Duck Creek, another replies.

Judy has also come outside. How are you going, Dad?

Okay ... Just having a stickybeak in the laundry.

I keep seeing *Babci* next to her peg bag whenever I go in there, I say.

Babci was like that, Dad ... You know, she liked colour. What about her embroidery, all those blouses and tablecloths she made?

And I know straightaway that I'm wrong — that the bag belongs precisely for the reason Judy suggests, and it's not out of place, that it was my mother's way of expressing herself and her life without making a formal statement about herself or her life. It's good to hear her refer to her grandmother as *Babcia* or *Babci*, the Polish word that my three children have used since they were able to speak, just as they still refer to my father, their grandfather, as *Dziadzia*.

It does not take long to mow the back lawns, such as they are now, the weeds proliferating. My father's efforts to keep them "clean", as he used to say, are vanishing after nearly five decades. For years after he retired from the Water Board at the age of 70, he would sit on an empty wheat bag, weather permitting, hat on, head down, and diligently weed the lawn with a small knife. When one blade wore out he would replace the knife. The pile of weeds next to him would grow and he'd move on to the next patch, and so on. By day's end, the mounds would be collected and thrown into the reserve behind our house. By week's end the back lawn was free of weeds. He would get up regularly for meal breaks, have a drink if it was hot and return to the yard — working steadily, methodically, never varying his routine in spring and summer when the weeds were at their worst. He would take out his handkerchief, dab his face, wipe the sweat from his eyes and brow, then continue working — as if hot weather and the act of wiping away sweat was unimportant compared with the weeding itself. When the back lawn was finished he would start on the front. Many times I would go out to speak to him, to bring a message from my mother or ask if there was something he needed from the supermarket, and I would stop, back off, leave the message or question for another time. He would be lost in a world of his own, seemingly oblivious to time and place, totally focused on the job at hand, and I knew it would be wrong to interrupt him, to awaken him from that state of mind or soul that he'd withdrawn into. You would find the dog next to him, or nearby in the shade of a tree, keeping him company, watching over the backyard of what could have been the mightiest kingdom on earth, such was the loyalty the dog displayed to his master and such was the reverence that the master exhibited towards his small plot of land, which he had worked since 1951. While he worked, my father had a phrase that summed up his attitude towards work: *moja służba*, "my duty". He didn't believe in taking days off work, or "sickies". Come what may, coughs, colds, a sore back or the 'flu, he went to work. In 1968 when he had to go into hospital for the removal of a cancerous growth on his foot, there was no getting out of going to his job. Years later, in his retirement, though he was too old to dig and plant, he regarded it his duty to keep the lawns weeded and cut, tidy. I have tried all my life to appreciate and respect my parents' love of gardening, of growing vegetables, fruits and flowers, which stemmed from their farming backgrounds in Europe and, such as it was, continued in suburban Sydney. Gardening was their way of perpetuating their European traditions in Australia, and giving their lives a meaning over and beyond what a daily job had to offer. Emigration had changed their lives externally, yet essentially they remained themselves.

I dump the grass cuttings into the chooks' enclosure, clean the lawnmower and store it in the garage. After my father died in 1994, my mother killed the remaining two hens and the chook yard was allowed to fall into further ruin. Today, overgrown with weeds, its wooden posts are half-rotted and the chicken wire sags between them. The stump of a giant oak is all that remains of the tree that fell during a hailstorm in 1991 and had to be cut up. The oak was grown from an acorn brought home from a tree in the garden of Dr and Mrs O'Brien, in Malvern Crescent, Strathfield.

Why don't you come inside now, Dad? Judy has come out with a drink for me. Let's watch a bit of the Anzac march.

How did the veranda come up? I ask.

Okay, she replies nonchalantly — with that same air of abstractness that my mother used to have when the question seemed to be of no significance.

Inside the house it is cool. I realise that I have not even been inside since I arrived. The laundry, garage and lawns took my interest. I have paid no attention to the house or what Judy's been doing. Besides cleaning the veranda, she's swept and vacuumed the house.

The Anzac Day march is under way.

My parents used to sit on the same couch that we're sitting on and watch this spectacle year after year. The names that the TV commentators read out are the same ... Borneo, North Africa, New Guinea, Vietnam, Gallipoli, World War I, World War II, Great Britain, the Commonwealth, United States of America ... Flags and bright banners, marching bands, old men and women, middle-aged men and women, grandchildren, very old ex-soldiers in jeeps and taxis, regiments, divisions, battalions ... A sense of *déjà vu* fills my head, an awareness of something other than seconds and minutes ticking away.

As a child I used to be impressed by such displays, by the nobility of great causes that we were told about at school. Soldiers saved countries from an enemy and one never questioned who that might be. Whatever parents, teachers or grown-ups said made sense and I acknowledged their superior knowledge. It was not until I went to Sydney Teachers' College in 1965 and had to study Alan Seymour's play *The One Day of the Year* that I started to question the validity of war, the purpose and senselessness of killing, no matter what the war or the country or who the enemy might be.

That year I also discovered the poetry of Wilfred Owen. Somehow, mysteriously, wondrously, the argument against war made sense. Poetry taught me that lesson: there is no argument to justify war. It was not one of the Ten Commandments that drove that lesson home, not a sermon from a pulpit, not hearing a parent or politician speak, but the voice of a poet, who himself was to die in war, who said plainly and simply, war is waste; it is wrong.

When I read "Strange Meeting" with its lines,
"Strange friend," I said, "here is no cause to mourn."
"None," said the other, "save the undone years,
The hopelessness. Whatever hope is yours,
Was my life also; I went hunting wild
After the wildest beauty in the world,
Which lies not calm in eyes, or braided hair,
But mocks the steady running of the hour,
And if it grieves, grieves richlier than here ..."

I knew that I had made a personal discovery, had stumbled across an important human truth, yet it was something so basic, so elemental, it was almost absurd. I knew that I could never support any war, ever again, no matter how glorious or noble the cause might sound, no matter what nations were at war, no matter how majestic the panoplies on display might be.

The early 1960s were years of conscription in Australia, introduced by the then conservative Coalition government. Nineteen-year-olds were called up for military service; many were sent to Vietnam and died there. I was in the first ballot and was called up for a medical. When I failed, I was relieved, but at the same time angry that my rights were not considered in the decision to call me up; it seemed that the whole deal was made by politicians for the expediency and benefit of politics itself.

The veranda has dried and shines like porcelain. My parents would be proud of the work that Judy has put into the house, a duty she has performed before and does so without being asked. Nothing is too much for her when it comes to helping me look after the house.

My parents helped me raise my three children by minding them when they were little. Judy, being their first grandchild, without being more spoiled than Andrew or Anna, made the initial impression on their lives as grandparents. No sacrifice was too big, no effort too much for them where she, or the others, were concerned. Maybe in them, I would like to think, they found a little of their own lives from the Ukraine and Poland.

In 1994, when my father was dying, Andrew and I gave him a bath. This "refreshing him", as my mother referred to it, included trimming his fingernails and toenails. It was a Friday. The day before, after examining him for chest pains, the doctor had offered to put him into hospital. My father refused.

I was there, next to him, but I gave the refusal no serious consideration. *He'll get better; he's pulled through before*, I thought. The next day my mother rang and requested that Andrew and I come over and bathe him.

During the trimming of his toenails my mother spoke to him, explaining what Andrew was doing.

That's not Andrew, he replied, that's little Peter's little boy.

He spoke in a clear voice, totally coherent, as if he'd walked in from somewhere else. Earlier in the day, he talked to my mother about the rye fields in Poland that he was running through, on his farm, when the Germans arrived in Raciborow and captured him.

It would be too easy to say that he was regressing, that his mind was already returning to its infancy, to "that other place", whatever people mean when they use that phrase. Yet I know that for my parents it was a reference to the Old World of Europe, with its inclusion of family values that contained the meaning of life itself — life as only they understood it. "Three for one and one for three." We lived by that motto after we moved to Australia. Now, decades later, it was my responsibility to pass it on, into the lives of my children. Love. Sacrifice. Self-denial … A list of do's and don'ts that was as prescriptive as the Ten Commandments. After all, the journey to Australia had been done for my sake as well as theirs, for a future in a country that hadn't experienced wars the way

Europe experienced them. My responsibility was now towards my children and their future.

You look sad, says Judy.

Nope. I've just remembered I was going to tidy up the
garage.

Want me to help?

No, no … Stay and watch TV or relax. Whatever you want.
Make yourself another cup of tea. This won't take long. I've let
things pile up there. The palms need watering and I'll put them
outside for a while.

A coldness passes through me as I enter the garage. This is a
different feeling than standing in the laundry and fossicking
through cupboards. This was, essentially, my father's domain,
the repository of all his tools, garden implements, a collective
of old pieces of timber, glass panes, hoses, saws. At the far end,
under a window, is his work bench, loaded with hammers,
files, tins and small boxes, jars of nails, screws, tap washers.
There are stubs of old pencils, pieces of chalk, crayons, whet-
stones, tangled clumps of string, copper wire, old paint tins,
bottles of mineral turps, machinery oil. On another table is his
collection of hammers, a tomahawk, screwdrivers, chisels, a
hand broom and dust pan, garden clippers and hand shears, a
Stillson wrench, a rubber mallet.

I take my two raphis palms outside and water them. They
never grew well in my house so my father agreed to take them
and see if they improved here. They did, as if both plants knew
automatically what was expected of them. Within a year they
had doubled in size. Their foliage deepened to a darker green
and the leaves broadened. When I quizzed him about his success he simply said they were in the right place, that he gave
them plenty of water and the garage must have had the right
combination of sun and shade.

If my mother had any claim to the garage as "her territory"
it was in the three clotheslines that had been strung from wall
to wall. What was hanging there when she died is still there. A

piece of green feltex, an old towel and a small quilt. Among them, coloured plastic pegs are spaced like distance indicators.

As I continue looking around, the coldness remains and spreads through me as if I had swallowed ice.

Under the bench, in the far left corner, is a large brown wooden trunk, its convex lid and sides reinforced with steel bands. My father built it in the camp in Lebenstedt. When we travelled to Australia many of our worldly possessions were packed into that trunk. There's also a smaller green trunk that my father built upon arrival in Australia. Inside, the timber is clean and yellow, fresh, like the wood had been sawn recently. On top is a steel bassinette, also brought from Germany. It was used to bathe me in the camps, as my mother was moved around with me. Next to these is my father's first lawnmower, a yellow Pope model, still in fair working condition, with its grass catcher beginning to rust.

Brooms stand upside down between the door and the roller shutter, millet brooms and hair brooms of all sizes, a pink cob-web duster. Opposite them, an old black-and-white Pye TV set that once belonged to me. In front of it lies the whipper-snipper that my father asked me to buy so that cutting weeds would be easier when he grew old; then he hardly used it.

The raphis palms are usually located between all this para-phernalia, in the coolest part of the garage, next to a small white stepladder that my father built. Meticulously measured, sawn, drilled, nailed, painted, it stands as a testament to a craftsman's art.

Other objects catch my eye and each of them is connected to a special memory, like the blue vinyl stroller that I used to wheel my children in to Rose Park, Sefton, when we lived in Chester Hill. I would push it up McClelland Street, across Hector, turn left and down Batt Street, across Rose and turn right, down a laneway, into the park. Hours were spent on the merry-go-round, the swings, the slippery dip, happy, fulfilling hours, thinking about the future.

Opposite the stroller, standing upright, is my mother's red shopping trolley. She would travel to Auburn or Bankstown or the local shopping centre for her purchases, fill the trolley to the brim and return home eagerly because she was coming back to her family to cook — something that gave her pleasure until the end of her life.

Between the stroller and brown trunk is my father's wheel-barrow, the kind I have never seen anywhere else, with its iron wheel and iron spokes, weighing a metaphorical "ton" and so strong it will outlive me. It is without rust. Clean. My father gave me rides in it when I was a little boy, up and down the rows of potato plants ... And for a moment I see myself doing the same with my children, piling them in one at a time, play-ing "doubles", around and around the backyard that is now grassed over. Bobby the dog is chasing us, the children are laughing, holding on to the sides. I'm trying to keep balance so that we don't topple over. Finally I have to stop, tired and sweating. The dog's tail is wagging madly, his tongue hanging out. My parents are on the back steps of the house, watching, shading their eyes from the afternoon sun.

The wheelbarrow is filled with small pieces of rolled-up carpet, tied together with twine in my father's inimitable fash-ion of securing things. He believed in the worth of twine and string. If it was strong, it was reliable, and you also needed to know how to tie it correctly. Beneath the rolls of carpet is a cardboard box with old Polish newspapers, yellowed with age, that my father refused to throw out. I know if I lift up the box, cockroaches and silverfish will scatter in all directions.

The new Masport lawnmower stands on a small platform my father built to keep it off floor level, just in case the garage flooded — as it did several times in the fifties and sixties when Duck Creek overflowed and water ran through our yard. It was only in the seventies, when Bankstown Council began a gradual but systematic widening of the creek, with a network of drains and canals further back towards Birrong, that the problem of flooding in Mary Street was alleviated. In the nineties, the street was finally kerbed and guttered.

On the floor beside the lawnmower is my father's edger that was bought for him. Trimming the edges of the lawns by hand had become too difficult because of the onset of a mild form of Parkinson's disease. His left hand would shake, sometimes more than at other times; it could never be really predicted. At first he was keen to use the edger, and tried valiantly, but by now he was into his eighties and starting it became a problem, or holding it steady to get the edges straight while the motor was running. Finally, in frustration, he gave up using it and reverted to the "shearing clippers" he'd used previously, holding his left hand at the wrist with his right, while he laboriously clipped and struggled with his left hand. Eventually, Mum and I talked him into abandoning the lawns altogether. Andrew became the "lawnmowing man", using the Masport mower, whipper-snipper and edger while my father supervised — walking alongside Andrew and pointing out patches of lawn he might have missed or standing in the background, watching.

Above me, between two rafters and laid on its side, is my Speedwell bicycle, in purple, green and white, its chrome rusted and peeling. My parents bought it for me from Bennet & Wood in the city, after the previous bicycle I'd owned was stolen from outside Chester Hill library. It was during my last year at high school and I'd ridden from Regents Park to return some history books. I parked the bike outside the main doors, turned my back for two or three minutes, came out and discovered my bike was stolen. I'd worked in school holidays, bred budgies and sold them to make money so I could buy that bike, as well as the accessories — headlamp, saddlebags, chain gears, reflectors, speedometer. A hard lesson in the security of property, and one I've never forgotten.

Outside in the garden it is sunny. The Anzac Day marchers had fine weather after all; now they will be celebrating in hotels, clubs, private homes, in the streets — saluting the flag, drinking toasts, getting drunk, yarning, remembering ...

Snow Is Falling

Snow is falling gently, softly, so fine and powdery it is like a mist.

This is my first memory of Germany.

Is this where I began?

No, it can't be because I have another memory, deeper and darker than all the nights of my life put together. I never used to talk about this memory, at least not for decades; it wasn't because I was afraid, but because I thought that nobody would believe me, that people would laugh and call me stupid.

The snow is falling against a windowpane.

Is it tapping?

I am three years old.

My nose is pressed against the cold glass and a naked light globe brightens the room.

This will be our last Christmas in Lebenstedt, Germany, in the Displaced Persons' camp where we have been quartered. From here we will make our way, via Austria and Italy, across the seas to Australia.

I am kneeling on a chair and looking at the drifting snow. Mounds of it are growing.

Directly beneath the window is a wire enclosure with a low wooden structure, like a dog's kennel, subdivided and lined with straw. That is where my father keeps rabbits. They are not being kept as pets; I am not allowed to play with them. These rabbits are kept for meat. They are bred, fattened and killed. Food in the camp comes from rations and food queues in the mess hall. There are people of all nationalities who depend on what is given out by the authorities, so many that often there isn't enough food to go around and satisfy everyone. People are forced to resort to other means to supplement their diet, their food supplies. Not only can we eat the rabbits, but we can sell the meat or trade it.

The snow is coupled with another beautiful element, but more dazzling, more transparent.

Light.

The word we associate with earliest childhood, even infancy, the word that enters our vocabulary as soon as we have some inkling about life itself. It blinds us when we are born. We associate it with the sun, fire, candles. We reach for it while still in our mothers' arms, turn towards it or from it when we first wake. It becomes synonymous with warmth, with illuminating the darkness. In the Bible it's an early part of Creation. "And God said, 'Let there be light', and there was light."

The snow falls from a blue sky so pale it resembles the frail shell of a bird's egg.

The snow falls from this clean sky and passes through light that radiates it even more; it turns the snow into a milky drift and a transparent sheet at the same time, but I can't see or touch the wind that blows the snow, just as I know it's impossible to touch the light.

My mother takes me by the hand and is going to bathe and dress me for the Christmas party being held in the camp's hall. We are having Christmas in Germany, among people like ourselves, while waiting for news of our application to emigrate to Australia.

Like us, they are living in hope.

Poles, Russians, Germans, Ukrainians, Hungarians ... Balts, Slavs, Gentiles, Jews. Single people and married people, children and babies, all destined for a New World, north or south of the Equator.

My nose, chin and mouth have left impressions on the glass, but my breath now clouds them. I wave goodbye to the rabbits and, with my mother's help, get off the chair. The time for watching the snow fall is over, but that other memory, my deepest secret, rises in my mind and then it's gone, like a dream that fades quickly. But it will return.

My long socks are woollen, thick and prickly, though they're not even socks in the strict sense of the word because my mother has knitted long johns. It doesn't take long to get used to the wool's prickliness, and the socks are warm. Singlet, white shirt, underpants, a blue velvet suit and short black leather boots complete my attire. My mother adds a silver pin to the lapel of the jacket, a bird in flight, sleek as an arrow. In every formal photograph I have of myself from Germany, I am wearing that pin, the bird in flight, like a talisman.

Two photographs in one of our family albums tell the story of that night.

Who took the photographs?

Another "Displaced Person"?

An official photographer? I doubt it.

Who in the camp was wealthy enough to own a camera and how did my family end up with the photographs?

In one photograph there are four children and seven adults, four women and three men. Two of these are my parents. I am one of the children. There are two other boys about my age. The fourth child is also young but it's hard to tell whether it's a girl or boy. Everyone is sitting at a long, rectangular table and has been positioned to face the camera. Food and drinks are laid out. The table cloth is white and appears to have been starched. I am sitting on my mother's lap, looking up at the ceiling. Had something caught my eye? The end of my collar is turned up, like an origami bird's wing. The other children stare straight ahead. One is smiling. Another, open-mouthed, appears startled. They are wearing what must be their best dresses and coats. One has a large white bib. A Christmas tree, festooned with streamers, baubles and stars, stands majestically in the background. All the adults look very solemn, are smiling gravely and seem transfixed by the camera. There is an air of seriousness about them that contradicts the nature of the occasion.

The other photograph contains just my father and myself and it has been cut out from a larger group photograph. Who cut it out? Probably my mother. Why? It's the same evening, yes, but my jacket has been taken off and I'm sitting cross-legged, left ankle over right, my hands clasped, left thumb over right. I appear to be pouting, bottom lip protruding, eyes again upturned, as if distracted or bored.

This is the photograph that always fascinates me, that I find the most revealing personally. To see a child running, at play, or being active, even smiling, is something worth remembering, worth capturing on film, but the inactive child, the one who will sit and say nothing, refuse to respond to an adult's question or smile for the camera, is seen as someone who is not worth wasting film on.

Yet there I am, just like that.

Just as I am today.

When I sit down and stretch my legs or sit with my foot under me, it's the left ankle that crosses over the right. When I clasp my hands, the left thumb goes over the right. My bottom lip sticks out when I consider a situation or gaze upwards to consider a question. How much have I essentially changed in five decades?

How much of what happened later that night has influenced my attitude towards drinking and given me a fear of drunks?

The small boy looking away from the camera is the same child who will shortly see a drunken man break into the hall where the party is being held and make a lunge for his mother. The drunk will grab her and attempt to kiss her. When the boy's father comes to her rescue the drunk will wheel about, throw the mother aside and produce a knife from somewhere and hold it to the father's throat, threatening to slash it if the woman doesn't go with him. All this the small boy remembers, and he will be told more of the story in later years, when he persists and asks questions about the photograph and his parents can no longer ignore him. His mother will tell him that he went "crazy" and screamed when the knife was held to his father's throat, that he screamed and distracted the drunk. Somehow, miraculously, the drunk was disarmed without causing any harm to anyone. Police arrived. He was taken away and put into a cell whose floor was covered in water so that he would sober up more quickly, so that he would never forget the nature of justice in a German cell.

We walk back in the cold dark, in the drifting snow.

Lights from the barracks have been turned off or down to a minimum, to preserve electricity. Those that remain along the paths create an eerie light that makes it appear we are walking on the moon's surface. There is no joy in seeing the presents that dangle from my parents' hands. I cling to my mother and bury my face in her neck. My father's arm encircles us, and both parents quicken their pace to get indoors quickly. My father keeps reassuring my mother that he is unharmed. He refers to her as *dziecko*, "child". He is twelve years older than her, and this is a term of endearment.

Except for the wind blowing against us and the buildings we're walking between, there are no other sounds. All sounds of Christmas have faded. No one sings *Cicha Noc*, and it will be a long time before I hear "Silent Night" sung in Polish. Next year there will be strains of it, but these will be intermingled with a new language, English, and though the melody will be the same, the feelings will be different because there will be no snow.

Our rooms are nearby and that means warmth and safety.

We pass by windows where lights are low or have been extinguished. I have learnt to distinguish between light from a globe and light from a candle. These are mostly lights from candles.

One by one, my thoughts fall into rhythm with their steps, and I realise my parents are speaking about the "new home" we will be sailing to. Soon, our application will be approved, they are saying. Or am I dreaming it? The new country is a safe country, without wars, where people can make their dreams come true. They have said all this before, but in the dark, and after the attack in the hall, there is tension in their voices.

Again they speak about leaving. The sooner the better, they both agree.

The snow sweeps across our faces, buries their conversation in the darkness that is Christmas morning.

I can hear very little, and I bury my face even deeper into my mother's neck, snuggle against her. She asks something, but I can't make it out.

The rabbits, my father replies. Ah yes, now, the rabbits ...

Water

The Red Sea was never red except at sunset. In the wake of the ship, the furrows of foam quickly turned from white to red, to dark blue and black. The further the ship ploughed into the night, the more quickly the red turned into black.

After crossing the Equator, passengers slept on deck because of the heat. Men lounged about shirtless; many wore shorts. Women wore summer frocks and sun hats. Children ran about in bare feet and sandals.

What did these people talk about? Did they discuss families that they had lost track of, mothers, fathers, brothers, sisters? How was the journey across the Red Sea to a new country meant to compensate for the loss of a homeland? Who was waiting at the other end of the sea journey to answer their questions?

In 1964 my parents bought a family car, an EH Holden, and, as neither parent drove, I became the family chauffeur. On one occasion we decided on a trip to Shellharbour, on the New South Wales South Coast, where I'd arranged to meet a schoolmate, Kevin Coates, and his parents. Kevin and I met in 1961 at St Patrick's College, Strathfield. We failed to matriculate in our first attempt at the Leaving Certificate but on our second try in 1963 we succeeded. Now we were in our first year at Sydney University, studying Arts, and thought this would be an opportunity for the two families to meet. A picnic by the sea.

No sooner did the ocean come into view as we drove down Mount Ousley, nearing Wollongong, than my mother began to complain of feeling seasick. *Seasick?* How could that be? The ocean was still miles away.

You can't be feeling seasick, Mum, I said.

I can feel the ship rocking. It's the voyage all over again. Oh glory be ... God help us!

It's in your mind, Mum.

Here I was, behind the steering wheel of a car that my parents had paid for, presuming to tell my mother what she could or could not be feeling.

I know what she means, my father said. I feel the same sensation if I look at the ocean for too long.

Impossible. You're both wrong.

For the rest of the day I listened to my mother complain about the bad time she was having by being so near the water. She sat with her back to the water. My father seemed to tolerate the situation more stoically, though I sensed that he, too, was uneasy at having being brought to Shellharbour.

They got on splendidly with the Coates family, however.

I failed to understand my parents' reluctance to accept the ocean as something beautiful, and in those early years of our migration I also failed to understand a deeper and more poignant reason to be drawn into associations with their exile; it had to with their loss, with the word *żal*. Literally, it means "sadness" or "sorrow" or "grief", but it has a depth to it that no English word can capture, certainly not in three letters. Anglo-Australians, especially literary critics and academics, often confuse it with sentimentality and a lack of irony in the work of European immigrants, failing to understand the deep psychological and emotional issues in the heart of the immigrant. In doing so, they reveal their own ignorance of the state of being of Europeans and sometimes display an inner fear of being demonstrative themselves, of exhibiting their own feelings, especially men, in public.

Żal is more than a description of a physical feeling; it is a heartfelt reaction, carrying the notion of profound loss and yearning at the same time; it belongs to the language of the spirit or soul, to an Absolute that is intangible.

The sea voyage was an experience my parents obviously preferred to forget. Crossing the Red Sea between walls of parted water may have meant salvation for the biblical Israelites, but crossing it for my parents was the severance of an umbilical cord that bound them to Europe, and in particular to Poland and the Ukraine.

It is twilight in Naples, the sky purple and growing darker; it is the evening of 16 October 1949 and we are boarding the *General R. M. Blatchford*. Ahead lies the Mediterranean Sea, the Suez Canal, the Red Sea, the Arabian Sea, the Indian Ocean, the Southern Ocean and finally the Pacific Ocean. We are about to step off European soil. I will return to Naples in fifty years. My parents will never return.

The gangplank is enormous and must be very strong to take the weight of all those emigrants, many of whom are dressed in suits and coats, wearing ties, scarves and hats, correct attire, as if they were attending an evening function; their worldly possessions have been packed into wooden trunks and suitcases, tied with belts and lashed with ropes, labelled and locked. They file on board and there is much commotion on the dock. Officials, bureaucrats from the Department of Immigration in Australia, are doing final checks, herding them towards the "chariot" that will carry them to the Promised Land, giving no indication of the stifling and cramped conditions that exist ahead. Why should they? These Displaced Persons are used to "roughing it". If anything, Australia has already done them a favour by offering food and shelter, and work for the men while the women stay at home and bring up the children. Everyone's efforts help to make Australia great. Arthur Calwell, Minister for Immigration under the Chifley Labor Government, has practically guaranteed it.

So the presence of water enters our lives once we step on to the ship. It is swaying, despite its size and the great weight of its cargo.

I can see people crying.

Neither of my parents is crying.

There is too much to be done. Too much excitement.

The finality of departure is overshadowed by the prospect of what lies ahead in the New Land. No one considers words such as "racism" or "bigotry" or "discrimination". The war supposedly brought an end to all that. Adolf Hitler was dead. The Holocaust was over. The Allies had saved the people of Europe. Sanity and Reason would prevail. This was a new beginning. Decisions had been made. Besides, weren't we the lucky ones? What about all those who had failed the medicals and been rejected because of ill health? There was nothing for us to cry about.

Nearly fifty years later I will visit the Australian Archives in Canberra and discover the nominal roll of the *General R. M. Blatchford*. I will read the documentation relating to the ship's departure and arrival at each port. When I find our names — father, mother, child — listed on page 22 and see our numbers (529, 530, 531) I will cry as if I had stumbled across an awful truth. This is not a secret about myself that I choose not to disclose. This is a fact about myself and somehow it helps me to understand just a little more of where I fitted into the scheme of things in 1949. The rest of the nominal roll reads like a statistic from the war that has no relevance to what is happening in my life today. Or does it? There was a total of 484 males on the ship; 402 females; 144 boys aged between two and ten years; 160 girls aged between two and ten years; 29 children under two years. Total: 1219. Where are those people today? How many of the boys and girls whom I played with on that ship are dead? What became of their lives?

Images of water continue to haunt me.

In the file of the *General R. M. Blatchford* I find the facts relating to another memory: the burial at sea of a boy named Jan Dul, not quite two years old.

The sky is grey, as bleak as concrete, and a wind sweeps the deck, bringing rain. The waves are choppy and their crests break into foam. We are in the Indian Ocean and the ship will be docking in Fremantle next. A burial service is being conducted. I see myself standing between both parents on an upper deck, holding their hands, looking down at people crowded on the port side. Flags are tearing in the wind. Suddenly a small platform is raised, at a steep angle, so that it resembles a slippery dip; it is held in that position briefly, an object slides off it, then it is returned to its horizontal position. The service is over. People want to escape the rain. We return to our cabin below deck.

As we climb down, I stare at the ocean with its hissing spray and granite-blue hardness, wiping rain from my eyes.

Illnesses were not uncommon on the ship and stops were made at Colombo and Perth to allow passengers who had contracted various contagious diseases to disembark; they were then taken to hospitals. Their families were also taken off the ship. At Colombo, in the inky blackness of the night, small boats pulled up alongside the ship. These boats resembled large, flat baskets with one or two people in them. These were sellers and traders bringing silver and gold ornaments, beads, spices, silk scarves and small black elephants. They wore strange clothes, white and loosely hanging, with their heads wrapped in what looked like towels. They spoke a strange language. We couldn't understand them, and they couldn't understand us. The water was flat, like polished metal, as the ship lay at anchor and the lights of Colombo twinkled in the distance. People sang on deck at night, just as they did when we crossed the Red Sea, or someone played a harmonica or piano accordion. They were wistful melodies, laments and love songs, underscored with an exquisiteness that somehow made me feel they belonged more to birds and sea creatures than to human beings.

No sooner did we leave Fremantle than I was quarantined with measles. The next port of call would be Sydney, a six-day journey, and there I would be taken off to hospital.

Watching from the porthole in the sick bay, I remember passing through the Great Australian Bight. The waves were mountains, peaked with foam, unlike anything we had encountered. My mother would visit me daily, smuggle in food that she had prepared, and spend as much time with me as was permitted. If I fretted at the thought of going to hospital, she would assure me that it wasn't going to happen.

By the time we get to Sydney most of your spots will be gone. You must learn to believe me.

The doctors will take me away.

No one will be taking you anywhere.

Her eyes were set, looking straight into mine, and although I failed to understand intellectually, I knew that she meant what she said when she spoke in that tone of voice. She would not break her word to me. That kind of determination must have helped her survive the years she spent alone with me in various Displaced Persons camps in Germany before she met Feliks Skrzynecki, who was to become my adopting father, in Lebenstedt, she and my biological father having separated before I was born.

Before the ship docked at number 13 Wharf, Pyrmont, I found myself reunited with my parents whether or not my traces of measles remained.

Our arrival was all too exciting, too important to allow other issues to overshadow it. There was much to be done by the bureaucrats. The refugees had to be dispatched to Bathurst, to the Department of Immigration Reception and

Training Centre. Trains were leaving that same night at 10 p.m., 11 p.m. and midnight. Escort officers would travel with the new arrivals. Luggage was loaded immediately in special vans; medical histories, X-ray photographs and Letters of Authority were being forwarded to the Director of the Reception Centre in Bathurst. Displaced Persons were bound under a two-year contract to undertake any work that was found for them in Australia, unless sponsorship had been arranged.

This was the experience of my parents and the hundreds of others who arrived with them on 11 November 1949. Their exile had been officially recorded into the annals of Australia's history. Not convicts. Not squatters. Not landed gentry. Just refugees — *reffos, wogs, dagoes, bloody Balts.*

The inscriptions on the back of our passport photographs read *Labourers for Australia*. I wonder if it read the same on the back of Jan Dul's photograph?

The Day that Lasted Forever

The camp in Bathurst was a former army training camp on the Lime Kilns Road outside the township; it consisted mainly of Nissen or "igloo" huts — long, semicircular sheds of corrugated iron that were an American innovation. After two weeks we were transported by trains and buses to Parkes, and it was here, during the next two years, that I would spend some of the happiest times of my life.

Parkes is the place that has left me with the most vivid and lasting memories of those very early days in Australia. It represents everything that Australia stands for as a country: the people, the land and its wealth, the wildlife and the extremes of climate, the fields of wheat, sheep grazing in flat paddocks or huddled in a flock under a huge gum tree, cattle, galahs clanging and wheeling over a farm and its homestead with willows or peppercorn trees, grain sheds and tractors … and a road of red dust and stones cutting through it all, east to west, but also leading to Sydney and the outside world, a road that I would travel on and never expect to return.

The two years at Parkes were spent in the knowledge that one day we would be leaving, though my parents never knew when that was going to be. That decision had everything to do with hard work, money and opportunity, just as it had to do with making a future for us in this new country.

My father left the camp and travelled to Sydney where he found work with the Water Board as a pipe-layer. He was a

labourer, "a pick-and-shovel man", and became a member of a
road gang that would be relocated to a different part of Sydney
every few months, but mostly in the outer, south-western de-
veloping suburbs like Bankstown and Liverpool. He lived in a
place called Tent City at the Water Board's depot at Pott's Hill,
between Birrong and Brunker Road, in Yagoona. Every
month he would visit us at the camp, stay a few days and return by train. For children like myself this was a thrilling time.
The day before the train arrived from Sydney we talked about
nothing except what we thought (and hoped) our fathers
would bring us. These ranged from boxes of chocolates, felt
toys, comics, Meccano sets, scooters, tricycles or bicycles,
spinning tops, games such as Snakes and Ladders, Ludo or
Dominoes, boxes of coloured pencils. Anything was a treasure
that arrived from that magical place called Sydney — far away
from the dusty roads, galahs and hot weather that we associated with the countryside around the camp. For us kids, the
distance was so great it could have been to the moon or Mars.

Parkes railway station consisted of one platform with a
wide roof arching over it, supported by long, curved steel
frames; it was both a terminus and a junction where passengers
changed trains for the Condobolin and Broken Hill lines.
Standing on the platform and looking east or west presented
one of the loneliest sights in the world. Although on the edge
of town, the sidings with shining crisscross lines cut across the
sleepers and blue metal. Grain would spill from passing freight
trains along the tracks and in the grasses that grew alongside
them. Standing on the edge of the platform was to be con-
fronted by an unreachable horizon, a landscape that shim-
mered in the heat, almost bare, as on the red-dust road that ran
in front of the camp.

The railway lines stretched, silver and metallic-hard, from
one distance to another. Joining one world to the next. And
there, on the edge of a cold grey platform (almost frosted in

winter, icy like the rails), I held my mother's hand and waited for my father's arrival.

Back in camp, while the adults sat around and ate, played cards and sang, we children played with what we'd been brought — pop guns and wind-up toys, marbles and dolls, all or any of those wonderful presents that we'd waited for so excitedly. In the evenings and into the nights, as thick clouds of cigarette smoke filled the barracks, we read comics and fell asleep behind a wall of voices, dreaming under black skies and golden specks of stars, ignorant of the time when any of us might have to leave the camp. We were just happy that our families were together.

Once, when my father returned, I learnt something about him that I never knew. His present to me was a white biplane, a Tiger Moth made entirely out of wood, without a single nail. Every piece of wood had either been glued or fitted together like a jigsaw puzzle. He even painted a red, white and blue RAAF "bullseye" on the wingtips. A roundel. The propeller spun in the wind when I ran and held it up. What seemed most wonderful of all were the wheels. Carved from wood! And two cockpits! My father had spent months of his spare time in Sydney carving and building this surprise. After he gave it to me, a neighbour from one of the huts snapped a photo of the three of us standing under a large gum tree, one of its branches fallen behind us, bark and weeds at our feet, My father is dressed casually, in an open-necked shirt, one foot forward, holding a cigarette, wearing a sleeveless jumper my mother had knitted for him. My mother wears a skirt, with a puffed-sleeved jumper in the Ukraine's national colours, three blue horizontal stripes on a yellow background. I stand between them, dressed impeccably in the same suit I wore at the Christmas party in Lebenstedt. My hair is combed neatly, in a huge bodgie-style wave. I am holding the hands of both parents, squinting at the sun. The Tiger Moth stands before me. My pride and joy.

The camp itself was a former RAAF Flying School whose facilities had been converted into living quarters for over 1000 immigrants. The gates were opened in 1949, when it officially became the Parkes Migrant Holding Centre. It had its own hospital, school, post office, dining hall and had the appearance of a small town — except there was a barrier, a boom gate, at the main entrance that had to be raised and lowered whenever a motor vehicle arrived or left. The "real" shops were in Clarinda Street, Parkes, the main street that cut the town in two like a wide river. That was where my mother took me shopping for new clothes, for ice-creams and lollies and any "extras" that we needed for our hut and weren't able to get at the camp.

For most of the two years that we lived on the town's outskirts, my mother worked as a domestic on various farms and in the town itself, including the house of the mayor, Mr C. J. Barber, in Gapp Street. A long stone and brick building with high verandas, it was the most impressive house I had ever seen. Neat lawns and beautiful front and back gardens surrounded number 6.

My mother took me with her to Gapp Street on one occasion, but when we arrived there we found that one of the Barbers's grandsons, Allan, was also there. He and I were to be playmates for the day, despite the fact that my English was still poor and I depended a lot on sign language. We were a surprise to each other, him with his long yellow locks and freckled face, me with my short black hair and olive features.

Disaster, straightaway, when I was told it was his birthday and his grandmother produced his present, a toy carpentry set. Hammer, saw, chisel, rule, pencil and nails. I started to bawl when he wouldn't let me play with it and continued when it was time to go home, even though he'd been persuaded to let me share it with him. We'd had a cake, lollies and cordial, and now I wanted to bring him back to the camp with us — or else for me to stay there for the night. I was led out of the yard crying, with Allan and Mr and Mrs Barber waving goodbye.

After dinner that night my mother and I went for a walk around the camp, as we often did. The night sounds of crickets and other insects followed us and echoed through the darkness. Noises crept down from the trees. Soft, rustling whispers. Frogs in the distance, creating a chorus. Stars twinkled as tiny jewels and the Milky Way streamed overhead like it was about to pour stardust over Parkes and the whole sleeping world.

My mother made reference to my behaviour in Gapp Street.

You must behave yourself. Don't be jealous.

But I want a toy set like Allan's got.

Not now.

Why?

I can't afford it.

When?

She shrugged her shoulders.

Maybe when your father returns from Sydney. But that's not what I want you to learn.

I don't want to learn anything. I just want what Allan's got.

That's exactly what I want you to learn.

What?

That you can't always have what you want.

I was angry with my mother. When she spoke like that I knew she was being wise; but I just wanted what I wanted.

Mum! I protested.

Look at the stars, she said calmly. Where I grew up in a village in the Ukraine we had mountains called the Carpathians. The stars were brighter than they are here. We were poor. Sometimes we cried because we were hungry and couldn't sleep, but we also knew how to love and laugh ... and we learnt to go without. We survived all that, and the war.

She started to hum and sing very softly as we headed back

to our hut, away from the forest and the empty space of what had once been an airfield.

Paddocks in the distance looked like they were a part of the moon, like the landscape of snow in the camp in Germany except that everything looked more grey, more silver. I imagined a small plane like my Tiger Moth droning over the hills, coming in to land, silver light reflecting off its wings, spinning off the propeller as it slowed down, the pilot waving from the cockpit. Moonlight was shining through him also, making him look like a ghost.

Whatever the lesson was meant to teach me, I knew it was over when my mother began to dream about her homeland. I knew that she missed it, but I never, never understood the depths of her homesickness.

Next day I was invited back to Gapp Street on the condition that I behave myself, whether Allan was there or not.

Before we entered the house through the back door, Mr Barber came out, followed by his wife who was holding Allan's hand. I stood back suspiciously. Why were they smiling?

Allan held out a wrapped present for me from behind his back. Even before I struggled to mumble "Thank you" and unwrap it there were tears in my eyes. Tears of joy, of embarrassment, of shame. I wanted to run away and hide from yesterday. I could see how surprised my mother was and she kept thanking the Barbers over and over. Allan took my hand and off we went into the backyard, bubbling with excitement, our minds full of ideas about all the things we were going to build. My last memory of Allan's grandparents was the expression of kindness in their faces. They seemed to understand what being a small child was all about.

My parents had said they would never return to Parkes once they left it, that they'd had enough of food queues and waiting at railway stations. Parkes lay at the end of a sea voyage, and their time there was coming to an end. After leaving, they had no desire to return.

But not me.

Living those two years in Parkes meant different things to them and to me. Whereas my parents remembered Europe vividly, I had only broken images of it: rabbits kept for food, snow falling outside a window, travelling by train through dark pine and birch forests that filtered sunlight and hid the scattered remains of bombers painted in camouflage colours that'd been shot down, boarding the *General R. M. Blatchford* at Naples, staring up at the huge gangplank for the start of the journey to Australia.

After a sea voyage of four weeks, Parkes meant open spaces, paddocks, sheep, cattle, gum trees, magpies stalking the ground on frosty mornings and throwing back their heads to sing. Parkes meant hot, dry weather, a bushland that I loved walking through, picking at branches of scrub wattle or encountering the scent of eucalypts for the first time. Parkes was where I saw a wedge-tailed eagle strung on a gate at Bartley's Creek — a property where my mother worked as a washerwoman and cleaning lady — and where I found a flock of sheep huddled under trees in the heat, rubbing their woolly rumps against the trunks, leaving fleecy threads in the bark and their droppings covering the ground; it was where I stood inside a split-slab hut, lost in the maze of harnesses that hung on its walls, under its cobwebbed rafters, brushing flies off my face; where I was thrown by a horse called Dodger that had been nicknamed Pig because he was so fat. Parkes is the origin of all these memories, as well as being the name of the township that gave its name to our first "home" in Australia.

Just as my parents remember what happened to them in Germany during the war, so I can remember, at least in part, what happened to me in Parkes, and I know that one day I will return.

Just as I remember coming home from school one afternoon several years later, after we settled into Regents Park in Sydney, and sitting on the back steps, waiting for my parents to return from work. I was watching sparrows hop around the garden, along rows of potatoes. Peewits were calling to each other behind the fence, in the bushes that grew around Duck Creek.

An unearthly feeling came over me, like I was about to fall asleep or become airborne into the afternoon light; I sat there, my knees drawn up under my chin, lost in a daydream. When I looked up I could see houses and factories on the hill that rises beyond Duck Creek and Jensen Oval, where Sefton ends and Chester Hill begins, where Virgil Avenue cuts the suburbs in half and dips over the horizon. A small boy ran across the scene and disappeared among the frames of buildings. He was fair-haired and freckled. Another small boy ran following him, dark-haired and olive-skinned. Both were carrying toy hammers and saws, laughing happily as they ran off, disappearing among the unbuilt houses and into the khaki bushland shadows. For a moment the sun blazed with a burst of brilliance as if it was morning, not late afternoon. I blinked, rubbing my eyes, staring in disbelief.

Billycart Days

He rode the red dust roads as a kid
in a billycart built from a fruitbox
along with other kids like himself
who lived on hope and laughter —
pointing their capguns at galahs and crows
that circled peppercorn trees
in a sky as blue as an exotic bird's eggshell.

Time was a never-ending road that ran
between Parkes and the rest of the world:
Orange, Bathurst, Lithgow —
the beautiful Blue Mountains
he remembered crossing once
in a train that blew smoke from its funnel.
Beyond them lay Sydney and its harbour.

Barefoot, head-down, pushing along
one of his playmates from the migrant camp
he'd laugh to see the billycart
go freewheeling down a path or hill
as others tried to pile in — squealing
as the wheels wobbled and they couldn't stop
because it didn't have a brake.

Dust in the eyes, dust in the mouth,
none of it mattered to them —
just as long as they were all together
at the end of those long hot days
and there was a drink of cold cordial for them.
It didn't matter who took the billycart home
because they'd all be back for it tomorrow.

Fifty years later none of it's vanished
because the red dust roads of Parkes
run like blood in his veins:
past the remains of the migrant camp
fenced off with steel posts and barbed wire —
whose concrete foundation slabs
lie broken and bleaching in the sun;

where thistles have been poisoned
so the site resembles a wasteland,
where there's no trace of the billycart
or the lives it carried around —
but where the surrounding hills echo
with the cries of crows, galahs, children's laughter
as fragile as an exotic bird's eggshell.

Strays

A pack of dogs lived around the hostel at Parkes; they wandered in from town or surrounding farms, roamed the empty paddocks around the airport that was once part of the Air Force Training Camp. They were strays, though some people wrongly called them "wild dogs". They were harmless and mostly went in search of food. Children befriended them. Whenever the chance presented itself, we played with them and fed them. Individually, they were fun, but when they hung around the mess hall as a pack, they posed a threat. There were big dogs, small dogs, mongrels, kelpies, cross-bred terriers, old blue cattle dogs, brown dogs, white dogs, black dogs, short-haired dogs, long-haired dogs.

I always wanted a dog, a playmate that was mine and would be there when my mother and father weren't. Dad was working in Sydney. Mum would be in town, cleaning someone's house, washing and ironing clothes, or she'd be out at Bartley's Creek doing the same for the Tom family. I'd be minded by one of the other mothers, Mrs Baran or Mrs Budzinski, after kindergarten in the camp, until the bus brought Mum from town. I reasoned that if I had my own dog to play with I wouldn't feel lonely.

Not all the men travelled out of the camp for work. Some with tradesmen's skills found employment on the site as carpenters, mechanics or general maintenance men. Others worked as translators.

One of these, Adam, became my friend. He wasn't married and was a quiet man. There were stories about his "real life" and who he'd lost during the war. He played cards with other men and smoked. He drank heavily.

Adam was a tall man and he was very strong. I used to call him Superman because I'd seen him bend a steel pipe with his hands. Sometimes I'd watch him as he sat and smoked by himself and just stared at the ground or up into the sky. I thought he looked lonely, sad. One of the dogs would come over and lick his hands, as I'd arrive on the way from school, and we'd pat the dog together and give it water from a tap that we'd collect in our scooped hands. Or I'd get up on the swings and he'd push me until I thought I was going to fall, even though I shouted *Higher! Higher!* Then I'd get the hiccups and we'd have to stop.

Adam worked as a carpenter but he was also an "odd jobs" man, a general assistant who was sent for when jobs needed doing. He could read, and I'd seen him translating letters from Poland for people who'd received them but couldn't read them. He was reliable, quiet, friendly, except when he got drunk. Then he'd become abusive, yell and curse, kick the dogs, cry.

On one occasion a child was bitten by one of the strays. Parents complained; they said they would deal with the animals themselves if the authorities didn't do something about the problem. Where was the particular dog that did this damage? Had the child provoked the animal? It didn't matter which dog, was the reply. The child only wanted to pat the animal. Remove the dogs, the men threatened, or we will kill them ourselves. If we cannot have guns we will beat them to death with sticks!

At that point the authorities decided that some course of action must be taken. But what? These were strays. Round them up, shoot them — that's what! Those that escape will taste blood in the wind. They will leave. And we have just the man for it — our general assistant, dependable, hardworking Adam.

Had he been in the room, the implied sarcasm in the reference to him would have been lost on Adam. Had he understood it, perhaps he might have even shrugged it off. What did it matter what they thought of him? Looking at the big picture, the total scheme of things in which he figured, the destruction of the dogs was of far less importance than the lives of men, women and children who had perished as a consequence of the tyrannical rule of Adolf Hitler.

You know how to go about rounding them up, Adam?

Yes, Mr Director.

Good. We'll provide a rifle when you're ready ... Just let us know.

Yes, Mr Director.

Jolly good. See you soon.

It took Adam only a day to convert the back of the truck so that it would hold the dogs. A cage had to be fixed, constructed of steel and wire, sufficiently strong to hold the dozen or so animals.

There was no way of predicting how the dogs would react once they were caged. There was also the problem of making sure that as many as possible were rounded up in one attempt. The best thing to do, he reasoned, would be to let them collect around the mess hall, park the truck nearby beforehand and entice them into it. Use scraps of food, bone. Get them into the cage. Drive into the bush. Kill them. No need to bury them. Crows and flies and ants would live off the corpses. Rain and wind and sun would do the rest. He'd already chosen the spot where he would take them.

Steel pipes, chicken wire and fencing wire were all that was needed to construct a cage on the back of the old army truck. Once that was finished, Adam began the job of rounding the dogs up. He walked, he whistled, he called and patted them, tricked them, one by one, into jumping into the cage. They growled and fought over the bones he threw in to keep them occupied. When he was satisfied there were no more, he raised the tailboard and locked it into place.

Strangely, he allowed me to help him. When I asked him why we were doing all this he explained that the dogs were being taken back to their owners. Some were on farms, some were in town. Some were even going to Forbes, some to Orange and even to Dubbo. These places meant nothing to me and I believed him. Finally, he sent me home, told me to go indoors and wait for my mother or return to whoever was minding me. He was on his way and would return next day — but as he got into the cabin of the truck I saw a rifle on the seat and asked him what it was for. His face changed, became red, and he screamed at me. Go inside! Do as you're told!

He slammed the door and started up the truck. The engine spluttered, coughed and turned over, and the truck moved forward with a jolt. It turned left, away from the mess hall where people had stopped to watch, then it turned right, towards the main road that ran to Sydney.

As if on cue, one after another the frightened dogs started to wail — long, hollow, pathetic sounds, out of trembling lungs and heaving stomachs. Barks, growls, yelps, all of these would be understandable, but those howls, those cries of pain, of abandonment, were so disquieting. They sounded chilling, almost human.

Children were asking questions.

Why are the dogs crying, Mummy?

Why's Adam taking the dogs away?

Why is there a cage on the truck?

My friend Superman had told me to go away but I was curious to see in what direction he would drive. Standing at the end of the main road, watching the truck drive off, I saw it turn left, and then a little way down the road, it turned right. There was a track that went deep into the forest. Adam had taken me for walks along it — to a creek where ducks bred and yellow wattles and white paperbarks grew. We used to throw flat stones along the creek and try to make them skim the surface. The soil was very sandy and red. When the wind rustled the trees it would also blow the soil.

I knew where the truck was heading and immediately ran diagonally across the camp, avoiding the road and the main entrance with its boom gate. Getting through the fence that ran around the camp's perimeter was no trouble, in fact it was fun. All the children knew where there were holes — or where it was bent because it'd been lifted so many times. Even an adult could crawl through.

Because the truck was going the longer way, and it was so slow, by the time I reached the main road it was only just ahead of me. Let him turn, I thought. Let him go down the road for a short distance. I kept to the side of the track, nearly in the bushes, otherwise I might be seen in the rear vision mirror. Half walking, half running, I managed to keep up with the truck. The dogs continued their barking. They snapped at each other. Some hurled themselves against the roof of the cage — as if the open sky represented a freedom they would never have again. The truck zigzagged. Was Adam playing with the steering wheel? Why didn't he drive in a straight line?

The truck came to a stop in a clearing, the same place that I remembered we'd visited before. The creek was further down, deeper in the bushes, but Adam was getting out of the truck and that meant he wasn't going any further.

The dogs became excited but in a different kind of way. Now they were wagging their tails and yapping happily. They were going to be released, let loose. Some were standing on their hind legs, pawing at the wire. They sniffed the air, licked it.

Birds that were singing fell silent. One. Two. Three ... I counted the seconds between the last magpie's song and its fading echo. Smaller birds, too, stopped their whistling and twittering. Even though the dogs were making a commotion, there was an eerie feeling in the air.

Suddenly I saw Adam lift a bottle over his head and throw it on to a rock. The sound of breaking glass was loud. The dogs became silent. You couldn't hear a single bird. Sunlight glinted off the clear glass. I realised it was the sort of bottle that the men in the camp drank vodka from. At the same time he began to swear, to curse, to kick at the truck, to menace and threaten the dogs with his fists.

One by one he took the dogs from the back of the truck and tied them to its side. Some of them came willingly, leaped down and licked his hand, wagged their tails. Others whimpered, refused to leave the cage; they were dragged out. The cage had been their prison; now it represented safety.

Let them go, I whispered. Please, let them go.

When I was leaving the camp to run after the truck I hadn't paid attention to what the children were saying to their mothers. Now I started to remember. Now I was feeling frightened.

What would Adam do if I ran out? Would he pay any attention to me and stop what he was going to do? He had taken his orders from the boss of the camp. He must carry them out. No, I couldn't run out.

There was nothing I could do except disappear, run back.

What would my mother tell me to do if she were here? She'd probably smack me for following a drunk man in a truck who was driving a pack of strays into the bush. Friend or no friend, that didn't matter. My mother loved me but she was also very strict. Rules were rules. Break them and you pay the price. Rule Number One After School was: don't wander away from the camp. Wait until I return from work.

Before I could decide, Adam reached into the truck and pulled out the rifle. He steadied himself, took out what must have been a bullet from his pocket, put it into the rifle and took aim. There was a sharp bang, a small puff of blue smoke and a dog leaped into the air as if it'd been prodded with an electric wire. It dropped dead beside the truck, its tongue hanging out in the dirt.

The rest of the strays began to whine, cry, tug at the ropes that held them. Some looked like they were spinning madly, doing a dance. Adam reloaded the gun, took aim and another dog yelped, jerked at the end of its rope, dropped into the dust, twitching as it fell. My heart was pounding like a hammer. I found it hard to breathe. There was a clawing in my throat. My jaws moved involuntarily. I thought I would vomit. My body shook with spasms but only saliva and hot air came up. I began to panic. I wanted to scream, to run, but my legs wouldn't move. They were frozen. I couldn't even close my eyes as Adam shot one dog after another — even when he finished and they lay there, a mass of fur and blood, dogs with their brains blown out and the pungent smell of gunpowder drifting in the air, killing the scent of the bush, staining the blue afternoon sky. Tears filled my eyes and I started to cry softly, like an animal myself, to whimper, burying my face in my arm.

Why did the man I called Superman have to do such a terrible thing?

He held the rifle up to the sky and started cursing; they were horrible words, Polish swear words. He flung his arms about, shook his hands and head as if he was arguing with somebody who wasn't there; and in between the words there was silence, hanging over the bush, waiting for his next outburst.

Tears rolled down my cheeks, onto my lips, my tongue. I tasted salt and saw the world through watery eyes; it was a liquid world. Everything was dissolving, merging. Trees became sky. Sky became trees. There was no distance between the truck and myself. The dogs were part of the red soil and the grass was part of the dogs. Sky. Trees. Grass. Dogs. Soil. A man with a rifle in his hands. The truck. The surrounding bush. Me. Everything was becoming something else.

Suddenly — suddenly there was a sharp snapping sound. Adam called out, Who's there? Hey, come out!

What happened? Did I tread on a twig? I turned around and started to run. What would he do if he caught me? He'd told me to stay away and I had disobeyed him. I kept seeing the dogs lying in a heap. How could he have done that to the dogs? He must have seen me because he called me by my name. Hey, come out … Don't be scared … I won't hurt you! But I was scared. Hurt me or not, I wasn't going back!

I turned around and started to run as fast as I could down the track. I heard birds singing, fluttering and flapping, their songs mixing with their wing beats. They were driving me on, pushing me away from the clearing, the presence of dead dogs, from the scent and sight of blood that I saw every time a bullet broke a dog's skull. In my panic I remembered a story the teacher had read at school about a flying horse called Pegasus. A magic horse. That's what I wished myself to be! Not even Superman could fly faster than Pegasus and I wasn't going to be caught! I pretended I had wings and they were now lifting me above the track. My eyes were blurred with tears and I was sobbing but that didn't stop me from running down the track, on to the main road and back to the camp. Before I reached the main road I heard another shot.

By the time I reached the boom gate I was sobbing and mumbling incoherently, panting like Pegasus would after a long flight over mountains and oceans. People took me to the camp's infirmary where Sister Fewtrell gave me a glass of warm milk and something to stop me from shaking and crying. She wrapped me in a blanket even though I wasn't cold. She sat by my side and held my hand, talked to me and stroked my forehead until my mother arrived. The police also arrived and talked to my mother, along with the Director of the camp. What was said I don't know, but for several days my mother didn't go to work and I was allowed to stay home and miss school. Whenever I asked questions about Adam or the dogs she'd just say, Shhh, shhh, go to sleep. Or, Don't worry, he's alright. But he wasn't at the camp anymore and when I persisted with my questions she told me that he'd been transferred to a different camp. Just like that, without a chance to say goodbye, I'd lost contact with my friend.

Years later, when we moved to Sydney, I overheard my parents and others speaking about the "terrible tragedy" of what happened to the man I called Superman, how he'd broken down under the strain of having lost his wife and two little girls in the war. All along he'd been telling people that he wasn't going to live "like a dog" anymore.

The Sewage Works

Friday, 16 March 1984
Parkes

The stagnant water is green, murky, its surface host to floating insects, mosquito larvae, bird droppings, leaves; it hardly seems to be water at all but rather a primeval sludge that has seeped from the earth into this rectangular concrete pit — two pits, in fact, separated by two walls, a narrow space between them also filled with the green water.

Crested pigeons make a wooden clapping sound with their wings and leap into a sky of molten blue glass. Galahs wheel in a circle from the red-dust road, protesting at my presence. The air is so hot it scratches the back of my throat. It hurts to breathe. Butterflies flutter in all directions. Grasshoppers leap ahead of me, through weeds and thistles, making sharp clicking noises. Flies whizz around maddeningly, sticking to arms and face. I should have brought a switch; instead I take out my handkerchief and wave it around, trying to keep them out of my eyes and mouth. Finally, after days of searching I've found what I was hoping to find, yet, for some reason, dreading the discovery: the site of the migrant hostel where I lived with my parents from 1949 to 1951.

I am thirty-nine years old and it's been thirty-three years since I was here last. For nearly four decades I've lived with memories and shards of memories that always return to one of three unforgettable incidents: my witnessing of the shooting of a pack of strays; an accident because of which a farmer will later have a leg amputated; and the death, by drowning, of a six-and-a-half-year-old playmate, Aleksander Hrubski, in one of the concrete pits.

This is my third and last visit to the former hostel site. Tomorrow I'm returning to Sydney. Each time I've come out from the motel where I'm staying I've failed to notice these sewage works. On the last visit, I notice a small speck on the horizon, at the western end, and I make my way towards it. What I find takes away my breath.

On one piece of machinery the letters WSL & D are moulded, and the date, 1939. Pipes run to and from it. A number of other above-ground structures, including a huge concrete pond-type construction with a central steel shaft, stands above them all. This is what I saw from a distance. As I drew closer, I saw it resembled a carousel. Another rectangular concrete tank has a ladder leading up to it. From the tank, a huge pipe runs out with a valve and tap at the base. Between these two constructions are the two "pits" full of the green sludge.

On 2 April 1950 a group of three children was playing near the pits, and one of them, Aleksander Hrubski, disappeared. According to newspaper reports in the *Champion Post*, the pit was eighteen feet deep and the accident occurred at 3 p.m. Police and migrant assistants failed to find the body by probing with long poles, so the Parkes Fire Brigade was called in to pump out the pit. In the early hours of the next morning the body of Aleksander was recovered.

In the accounts of those who witnessed the recovery, he lay at the bottom on his side, as if he were asleep, his hair washed back, looking like an angel. I will discover these details later, in 1999, when I return to Parkes to research another memory that has haunted me since 1951. But why does the description of that scene imprint itself on my mind with such horror? Is it because I used to play with him? Why did the authorities leave the sewage works open to trespass by children? As I stand in the sun and stare at the stagnant water's harsh green glare, I no longer bother to brush away flies. I've become accustomed to them, the dry heat, the thistles and dust.

My mind is elsewhere, in a landscape of snow, in Germany.

Night has fallen.

The room I'm floating in is small, lit up by a single light. My brown balaclava is on the floor; it is dirty and smells of excrement. All my clothes are dirty and have the same smell. I've been laid out, face down, on a table and several people are crowding around me. A man is frantically pressing down on me, pleading with me in Polish to breathe. A woman is crying.

I am dying.

But where is my mother?

I am dying and I want to see my mother.

Where is my mother?

I am becoming an angel, a spirit, floating into a light that is not coming from the globe but is everywhere; it is very strong. I am happy. I want to go into the light, but first I want to say goodbye to my mother. Where is she?

The door of the room bursts open and she tears in, screaming for me, pushing people aside, sobbing and crying all at once; it is heartbreaking.

How can I go into the light and leave her like this?

She turns me over and puts her fingers into my mouth, clearing out the muck that is in my throat. The man in the room is saying, *He's still breathing. The balaclava saved his life. It stopped his mouth filling up.* My mother's shawl has fallen off. There is snow on her face and hair. She went out gathering firewood and left me in the care of the other woman.

The light starts to fade, to release me from its power. I start to come down, to enter my body again. It was wonderful to be floating above those people, above the rectangular table that had been scrubbed and is now covered with waste from the cesspool that I fell in when I wandered out into the winter dark, looking for my mother. A stranger, a woman, alerted the woman who was minding me, telling her how she saw a small hand disappearing into the cesspool. My mother will recount this story over the years to me and swear that she never discovered the name of the stranger; it was like the lady had vanished into the snow.

When I begin to splutter and cough, to spit out the dirty water, it is certain that I will live. The woman minding me apologises profusely. The man is now comforting her. Other people have entered the room.

My mother wraps me in her shawl and carries me back to our quarters. She is sobbing, crushing me against her. I feel exhausted, very sleepy, but I would like to tell her about floating in the room and the bright light. Later she will return to reclaim the balaclava.

All this happened in Lebenstedt when I was two years old. Feliks Skrzynecki had not entered our lives yet. From that night on, my mother never let me out of her sight. Wherever she went, I was brought along. Even when she worked in Parkes, and I was allowed to go with her, she would say, *Play where I can see you.* Then she added, *If you disobey me, you'll get smacked.* She trained me like a puppy.

There are photographs to be taken, to visually record the site.

I quickly snap eight shots of the sewage works, from different angles, knowing there will never be a better time to do this. In 1988, when I return with my mother for a reunion as part of Australia's bicentenary celebrations, there will be hundreds of people here — former inmates of the camp, locals, councillors, politicians, visitors from all parts of Australia. People will crowd around the camp site, everyone with a different story to tell.

There is a fence around the sewage works, and a little way off, to the west, a farmhouse; its roof shines silver in the sun.

Should I go over, ask questions? See what else I can discover? Without looking back, I return to the car.

But it is impossible not to see the site from a distance, even as I start the ignition and prepare to turn the car around, back to the main road. Impossible not to see Aleksander playing by the edge of the sewage works, standing up and looking towards me, shielding his eyes, waving goodbye, then returning to play as if I never existed. Impossible not to see the broken concrete slabs, the steps and foundations shimmering in the heat, through the tall weeds, behind the red dust that skirts the road. Crows are flapping overhead, very low. The site resembles an old cemetery.

I return to my motel feeling physically exhausted and mentally emptied. That night, unable to sleep, I drive around Parkes — several times up and down Clarinda Street, past Fosseys and the Paragon Milk Bar, up to the post office, the court house and hospital, to the houses in Gapp Street and Hedgerow Avenue, both of which I'd visited earlier and where my mother had once worked.

On top of the War Memorial a blue light burns in memory of all those from Parkes who had died in various wars. From this lookout, I get a view of Parkes that, at night, could have been any country town. Lights also burn in outlying areas and along the highway. The stars are so numerous, so bright and clear. The scene below me, lights and houses, shops, stars and streetlights, farmhouses in the distance, the countryside, seems to have a quieting effect on me and I return to the motel.

I sleep soundly and find myself in the hut of the Parkes camp where I lived with my mother; it is late and she has returned from her English class.

I learnt more language exercises, she says proudly.

She is making herself a cup of tea and heating water over a kerosene primus she keeps on a shelf.

I don't care. Why must you go?

I want to learn the language quickly. I can learn it at the

places where I work — but this way I can have extra practice in the evening. How does this sound?

I don't want to listen.

When I say O my mouth goes so ... O ... O ... O ...

That's silly.

Or, one man went to mow, went to mow a meadow. Two men went to mow, went to mow a meadow ...

By now she has adopted a sing-song voice and is half saying the words, half singing them.

They teach us things like that. It makes us get used to English sounds. They show us a picture of a big ship like the one that brought us to Australia and say, This is not a sheep, it is a ship ... You try it.

Don't want to! I say emphatically.

Have some hot tea; it's nice and sweet. I've put in lots of sugar.

All right.

Soon I am cuddled against her, warm in bed, sipping tea from a big white enamel mug.

She asks, What did you learn at school? This is a reference to the preschool centre I attend in the camp.

Another nursery rhyme.

What's it called?

It's called "Humpty Dumpty" and it's about a giant egg that falls off a wall.

How do you know it's an egg?

Because the teacher said so.

So I proceed to teach my mother what I'd learnt that day, with appropriate hand actions, even plopping my head forward, rolling it from side to side, demonstrating that Humpty Dumpty was really dead. We both laugh, but by now I am yawning, unable to keep my eyes open.

Sleep, little man, sleep. My mother begins to sing a lullaby in Ukrainian, rocking me gently from side to side, breathing over me, giving me a goodnight kiss.

As I fall asleep, it isn't the words of "Humpty Dumpty" that repeat in my head; it is the sound of my mother's voice from a few minutes ago, *One man went to mow, went to mow a meadow. Two men went to mow, went to mow a ...*

I wake up startled, as if from a bad dream, and make my way in the darkness to the window.

This is my last night at the Bushman's Motor Inn, and here I am, again, unable to sleep.

There is nothing to see of the road or trees, only the night sky, bright with stars and oblivious to my restlessness.

What would my parents say if they saw me here in the dark, trying to make sense of a past they'd wished to forget. My father would shrug his shoulders, as if it didn't matter that I'd come here. When referring to matters of the heart, my mother often quoted the first line of a Tab Hunter song from the fifties, *There's no fool like a young fool ...* And this, I think, would be her judgment on the present situation, even though it doesn't have anything to do with the heart or love matters. Nor was I "young" any more. But I knew she wouldn't condemn me, either. I have to do what I have to do, whether it makes sense or not.

Migrant Hostel
Parkes, 1949–51

No one kept count
of all the comings and goings —
arrivals of newcomers
in busloads from the station,
sudden departures from adjoining blocks
that left us wondering
who would be coming next.

Nationalities sought
each other out instinctively
like a homing pigeon
circling to get its bearings;
years and place-names
recognised by accents,
partitioned off at night
by memories of hunger and hate.

For over two years
we lived like birds of passage —
always sensing a change
in the weather:
unaware of the season
whose track we would follow.

A barrier at the main gate
sealed off the highway
from our doorstep —
as it rose and fell like a finger
pointed in reprimand or shame;
and daily we passed
underneath or alongside it —
needing its sanction
to pass in and out of lives
that had only begun
or were dying.

The Circular Saw Accident

Sunday, 21 February 1999
Parkes

Again, fifteen years later, I've booked into the Bushman's Motor Inn. Although it's late summer, the weather is still hot and dry. The drive from Sydney, including a lunch stop in Lithgow, took four hours.

The 1984 trip was made in response to a persistence of memory, an attempt to come to terms with certain incidents that had affected my life, but there was something else, something that burned at the back of my mind and had never really stopped troubling me, something that happened and, except for general statements from my mother, of which I was never told the details. Because Parkes figured so strongly in those early years of my life, and because I regard it as my first home in Australia, it seemed imperative that certain traumas that I had experienced should be resolved.

One of the highlights of that first trip was re-establishing contact with the farming family, the Toms of Bartley's Creek, for whom my mother had worked. While I'd spent a pleasant day with the three brothers on one of the properties that Bartley's Creek had been subdivided into, there was something that still nagged me, something that I felt needed confronting. It had to do with painful memories, but it also had to do with the heroism of three men, the farmers who, fifty years ago, were young men and now, through a set of completely different circumstances, had come into my life again.

Having made the appropriate telephone calls from Sydney, having told the three brothers the reason for my intended trip, and receiving permission from them to visit, I arrived in Parkes.

Now, as I dived into the motel's pool in order to cool down, I felt as if I were plunging into the deep end of something distant. In the hot air of the central west the water felt very cold.

Monday, 22 February 1999
"Araluen"

I'm in the kitchen of Dorothea and Andrew Tom, the middle brother of the family. Their son Gavin is also at home and we meet when he comes in for morning tea. Outside, cockatoos are screeching. As Andrew speaks, I picture the red-dust road that runs off a bitumen road on to the property and the clouds of dust that my car has turned up rising into the blue sky. It's a long road, beginning at a cattle grid under an old gum tree, just as it was when I came out here as a little boy. Today, Bartley's Creek has been subdivided into three properties and this one, "Araluen", belongs to Andrew.

He begins by telling me that the incident whose facts I've returned to discover occurred when the brothers came home from boarding school in Sydney. They were working with their father, clearing land, using a newly bought mobile circular saw. He stresses how dangerous the machines were and that no instructions came with them. He explains minutely the mechanical principles on which they worked.

As a six-year-old I had accompanied the brothers and their father in an old blue Bedford truck to where they were cutting down pine trees for posts. Andrew was working the saw. A tree started to fall and the saw jammed; their father went in to lean against it, as did the other two brothers, Peter and

Warwick. As they did, the blade shot out of the tree. How it missed their father he can't say, but the blade flew out and "just cut them down like a couple of saplings". At first their father noticed only Warwick and, using his belt, tied a tourniquet around Warwick's knee. Then he saw that Peter had been injured also.

Andrew apologises to me for the haste with which everything happened from that point on. I had to be kept in the truck while paddock gates were opened in the headlong race to the homestead so that an ambulance could be called. Shock. Confusion. The uncertainty of what had actually happened to the two brothers. Peter was cut across the backs of both legs. Warwick lost a leg.

Andrew tells me of the complications that Peter has had up to the present, although he, like Warwick and Andrew, has made a success of his life, has married and raised a family. Warwick, whose hero, he says, was Tin Legs Bader, has achieved a lot also. He married, had a family, went on to get a pilot's licence and a commercial rating. Their father, he says, never talked much about the accident and somehow blamed himself for it.

The brothers were raced to hospital and given blood transfusions. Warwick, especially, had lost a lot of blood and it seemed like he wouldn't last the night. Andrew admits that he felt "rotten" because he "was on the saw". He says it took him ages to get over it. When people used to ask questions about the accident, all he could do was say nothing.

We continue talking a little longer. I share with him the stories of Aleksander Hrubski and the shooting of the strays. I describe the sewage works as they are today, still uncovered, full of dirty rainwater.

He talks with a farmer's stoicism about living on the land and the acceptance of life and death, the need to kill and destroy rodents, and the need to slaughter for meat rationing and how not to look into a sheep's eyes when you are cutting its throat.

We discover we have an interest in Australian birds and exchange stories about our experiences with them.

Dorothea returns from town and I'm invited to stay for lunch. I decline the offer but promise to return before my departure for Sydney.

Cockatoos screech outside, as if to scold me, warn me about overstaying my visit. They are saying that I am an intruder, that I must leave, that I have no place here anymore. The sky belongs to the birds, the land to the animals and these country people.

At the Parkes *Champion Post*, the file for all the newspapers from 1951 is missing. The newspapers are stored in a back room, on deep shelves, like groceries, inside large cardboard covers; they resemble giant scrapbooks. The office staff is helpful, but no one can explain why everything from 1951 is missing.

I drive over to the local library and find what I am looking for on microfiche; however, when I try to photocopy what I need, the photocopier won't work because it's out of toner. The chief librarian tells me that it's been ordered from Bathurst and assures me it will be here tomorrow afternoon.

I still have one more visit this afternoon. I make a telephone call and arrange it. It's well past lunch time but I'm not hungry.

Maria Dziuba works in a local nursing home. Her family and mine became friends on the voyage to Australia. She was one of my playmates at the migrant camp but her family stayed in the district when the camp closed. Fifty years later, she lives with her mother and one of her brothers in a street that is less than ten minutes' drive from the site of the former camp. My mother re-established contact with the family several years ago and we've stayed in touch since. Maria knows that I want to interview her mother about life in the camp. The visit to the nursing home will be short and has been timed to coincide with Maria's afternoon tea break.

We meet in an office where a receptionist has asked me to wait. I've met Maria before and there's a bond between us, a link because we've shared part of our childhood in Parkes but also, I think, because our mothers came from the Ukraine. I've seen the two women together and there's something intuitive between them, a bond also, but deeeeper, unspoken. Their dialect is the same, the vocabulary they use and their manner of speaking — even the hand gestures.

Maria shows me around the grounds of the nursing home and I tell her about today's interview, that there are still two brothers and her mother to interview.

Elderly people on walking frames and in wheelchairs pass by us. We look into a large room where afternoon tea is being served to residents sitting at a long table. The gardens are full of bright flowers and trimmed bushes. Neat lawns decorate the spaces between buildings.

She sees me out to the front garden and we make a time for me to visit her mother. The sun is starting to set and there are elongated shadows on the rectangular lawns.

It's well after four o'clock when I return to the Bushman's Motor Inn.

Tuesday, 23 February 1999
"Kimbar"

The directions to Mary and Warwick Tom's property take me along a different route from the Bartley's Creek Road. I travel down lower Clarinda Street and turn off at the Eugowra Road. Travelling along it I pass by the racetrack and the bulk grain terminal, and drive over a railway crossing.

As I make my way down the turn-off to the homestead, across paddocks wet with dew, Red Angus cattle watch me warily. At one point I have to slow down and pass among a group of these beasts that have come out of the trees and right up to the track. They peer at the stranger. There is something primeval about the shape of these animals. Their huge, humped shoulders denote tremendous strength. They are bigger than my car and their faces gloom frighteningly into its interior as I edge forward, metre by metre.

Mary and Warwick meet me at the door and we exchange greetings. I've never met Mary before; Warwick looks exactly the same as he did in 1989 when Mum and I returned to Parkes for the Migrant Camp Reunion. Warwick speaks while Mary serves tea and biscuits.

He admits he didn't have much to do with the migrant camp — although he remembers going out to it in the utility truck to pick up my mother in the mornings and return her in the afternoons. He remembers the exact route, however: he'd go by the Eugowra Road or else along the Back Yamma Road.

We discuss the exact dates of our arrival and departure at the camp, the death of the "little boy" in the sewage works and the date of the drowning, Monday, 3 April 1950. I refer to the photocopy of the newspaper I obtained when my mother and I returned for the Migrant Camp Reunion.

He doesn't remember the drowning, but realises it would have been before the accident.

We talk about none of them having met my father and how my mother used to find work in town with certain families: the Brownhills, the Ahrenses (Mrs Ahrens was the English teacher at the local high school), the Burnses, and the Barbers.

His account of the accident is less detailed than Andrew's, although the facts are much the same — the pine trees being cut down, Peter and him pushing on the tree over the saw's blade because the tree had "started to come back a bit". A gust of wind brought the tree back against them and the saw jumped out, spinning "at full throttle". Peter turned around and was struck from behind. Warwick pulls up his trouser leg and show me his prosthesis and the scars made by the saw's teeth. His voice is without sadness or regret. He says his leg is bearable and he has progressed with his life. He healed quickly because the cut was clean. Over and done with.

We talk a little longer, and before we say our goodbyes I ask Warwick and Mary if I could have a photograph of them in their front garden. They agree and stand in front of a cypress pine that's been clipped. As I line up the camera I realise it's as perfect a day as it could be. Any feelings of *żal* that emerged while Warwick spoke have been dissipated and I can't help blessing these people for sharing their lives with me. The light is clean, warm and cold at the same time. There's a purity in the air that's more than invigorating. My body feels it, my bones, my blood. I feel like I've come to Parkes for the first time in my life.

I go for a drive out to Eugowra and Forbes, where I have lunch. Back in Parkes, I visit the Henry Parkes Museum and buy a pictorial history of the town in a small bookshop in Clarinda Street. Again, I go for a swim at the motel. Back in my room, with images of the countryside drifting in and out of my mind, I fall into a deep sleep. There are two more interviews to be done.

Wednesday, 24 February 1999

I spend the morning shopping and sightseeing around Parkes. After lunch I drive out to the home of Mrs Maria Dziuba, Maria's mother, in Russell Street. All the while it's hard not to be drawn back to what Andrew and Warwick have told me in the last two days.

Maria and her mother show me around the large garden with its vegetable plots and fruit trees. There are chestnuts, pears, apples, oranges. Grape vines trail over wire fencing. A number of sheds and outhouses have been built in the yard. This agrarian scene reminds me of where I grew up in Sydney.

Both places have an atmosphere of rural antiquity about them. Both were created by people who emigrated from the Old World.

Walking inside the house is like entering a fairyland cavern of glass and porcelain, silks and beads. There are literally hundreds and hundreds of dolls, vases and trinkets of every imaginable size, colour and shape in cabinets and on shelves in the hallway. We sit in the lounge room on a couch covered in embroidered rugs and bright cushions. There are pictures and brass rubbings on the wall. A cuckoo clock and a painting of a river scene look familiar. Below them, a mock jade-and-sapphire peacock look backwards over its tail and screeches in silence.

We arrange ourselves in the room. I switch on the cassette recorder and ask Mrs Dziuba to tell me about life in the migrant camp.

What do you remember? I ask.

Her three Pomeranians share the room with us and they immediately start yapping. Mrs Dziuba reprimands them and they stop their commotion. When something else disturbs them they will start again. This will happen all the way through the interview.

What do I remember? Oh, I remember a lot ... about how people lived, how they went to the kitchen for food ... I witnessed a lot ... I didn't like what they did in the kitchen ... They stole food for themselves, but when you came into the kitchen they didn't want to give you food ... Like the time I said to the chef ... I tell him the bread is old, and he says for me to soak it with a bit of water and it'll be alright ... It was New Year, the men had returned from work ... They were giving them potatoes but not fresh bread. There was bread ... but he was giving them bread that was too hard and couldn't be cut ... So I got to the lock in the pantry in the kitchen where the bread was and opened it with a leg from a seat and got half a loaf of bread ... I took what I was entitled to ...

I ask her if she remembers the boy who drowned.

Yes, I remember.

Whose fault was it?

I don't know but ... Did you know his mother came back after ten years and they took his remains and buried him out near Liverpool somewhere?

She asks me, *Do you remember the Polish fellow in the camp who drove the truck to and from the station with the baggage? He drove the truck over the bridge. Do you know which bridge I mean? No? Well, it collapsed and he was killed ... He had something like eight children. They buried him here but his wife and children moved to Melbourne ... Later they dismantled the bridge and built a new one.*

I mention the killing of the dogs and she goes into details about the circumstances of the killing, how it was precipitated by complaints — from one woman in particular. The dogs were bothering children. I tell her how I heard that they were strays and were responsible for killing sheep in the district. Does she have more details? And what happened to the man who did the actual shooting? She said there was a terrible accident afterwards and people kept quiet about that trouble.

But there were other kinds of trouble too ... The men would fight a lot ... Yes, there were lots of fights and the men would hit each other ... and they yelled a lot ... We also had trouble with the young Australian men who came to the camp and wanted to get to the women ... One woman set a trap for them ... and then ... Oh boy, did we get stuck into them ... They cried and said they'd never return, and they never did ...

She talks about the difficulties of raising children in the environment of the camp, and the problems of cooking for them.

I used to have a small stove there and spent most of my time sitting by it and cooking for the children ... Oh yes, did I ever work hard and tire myself out ... All sorts of cooking ... Cabbage rolls, dumplings, pancakes, apple cakes and doughnuts ... Also I made my own meatloaf ... I used to cook it all up for Christmas and be visited by one or two Australian families and have a chicken also ... They always wanted me to give them my recipe but I said that I couldn't because I don't have one, that I just cook as I have a taste for something ... I said that even if it's in the fridge for three or four weeks it doesn't go off ...

Then we had troubles with accommodation ... New arrivals would come to the camp and there wasn't enough room ... Oh I had troubles with that ... So I found this little house and we moved into it ...

Mrs Dziuba goes into minute details about the purchase of her home, the size of its rooms, extensions, the previous owner. She speaks about families from the camp who settled in the area but who, once their children grew up and moved out, ended up by following them.

She also tells me that my mother's father was a Hungarian Jew and she received the name "Kornelia" from him. Did I know that? No, I tell her, not about the name-giving, but my mother had told me about her father without going into details about him. I tell her that it wasn't something that greatly interested me when I was growing up. It was never an issue then, though I do wish now, regretfully, that I'd asked more questions and learnt more of my mother's story.

She sees me looking at the cuckoo clock and the painting of the river and starts to laugh, asks me if I recognise them.

Your mother gave them to me but said not to tell you because you'd be upset.

The penny drops and I remember the cuckoo clock that'd been taken down because it'd stopped working, and the painting bought at a rummage sale and hung behind the laundry door. Mrs Dziuba and Maria once visited us at 10 Mary Street and my mother must have given these things to them at the time. I can't help but laugh. The dogs start yapping.

Her narrative becomes less a description of life at the camp and more of a personal history, a recounting of her own life in Germany and the Ukraine, her mother, her father, her siblings, her husband, her marriage and the birth of her children, their schooling, finding work, the difficulties she's having with her health in old age. Again and again we have to stop because of the dogs.

I sense that the interview is coming to an end and describe my recollections of the journey on the *General R. M. Blatchford*. I tell her that several years ago I researched the ship's file in the National Archives in Canberra and read the nominal roll and the paperwork dealing with the ship's journey.

She asks if there was anything about the rape of a young Polish woman by a gang of crew members. No, I tell her. There was nothing about that.

No, there wouldn't be. The captain said he'd fix it up ... It was terrible what they did to that poor girl ... terrible.

Maria interrupts and asks her mother to recount what happened when the ship docked in Sydney Harbour.

We were near Manly and everybody was calling out, I see land! Land! You could see Sydney on the left side ... There were little trees ... We had to stand for about an hour, then another hour ... It was about nine or half-past at that point ... Then we moved on and it was about eleven o'clock in the morning and then we stopped and waited ... and we arrived near the Harbour Bridge ... By the time we stopped again it was about four o'clock and they told us to clean the ship before we left ... Well, it was about ten or eleven o'clock before they finally let us off the ship and the buses arrived to take us to Bathurst.

Before I stop recording we have touched on the arrival of our two families in Sydney and the journey to the Bathurst

Migrant Holding Centre where all of us stayed for two weeks before being moved on to Parkes. After Parkes the two families were separated, the Skrzyneckis moving to Sydney, the Dziubas remaining in Parkes. Ironically, fifty years later, the stories of their lives are being joined via the medium of electromagnetic tape, turning very slowly, recording sounds, words, memories. Everything seems to be coming together, piece by piece, not always making sense but at least recognised as being related to our lives. Even the yapping of three small dogs doesn't seem out of place.

Thursday, 25 February 1999
"Bartleys Creek"

The last of my interviews in Parkes. Tomorrow I return to Sydney. Much of what Mrs Dziuba said yesterday circulates in my head. The reference to my maternal grandfather and his being Jewish was a surprise. How much of her life had my mother told her? And what am I to do with this fact? How do I incorporate it into the rest of my life from now on?

In town I purchase various gifts that I want to give to the three Tom families and Mrs Dziuba before I leave.

I first drive out to "Araluen" and say goodbye to Andrew and Dorothea. I leave them a gift and ask them to pass it on to Warwick and Mary, neither of whom are home today.

They agree to be photographed and stand under a trellised grape vine, its leaves a deep green, under which a wind chime has been hung.

Dorothea's glasses are slung around her neck. She is smiling a countrywoman's smile, warm and welcoming. Andrew stands with his hands in pockets, looking stoic and detached, as wise as any Greek philosopher, as if to say, I have seen it all, the good, the bad, the happy, the sad. I haven't noticed before how tall he is and think he must be very strong.

*   *

The "Bartley's Creek" homestead is painted pink and green, set inside a circumference of trees and shrubs. There are palms, climber roses, wisteria, variegated creepers trailing over walls and windows. One could be forgiven for thinking this was part of rainforest country, not the central west of New South Wales. When I visited with my mother in 1989 I remember there were many paintings and books in the rooms — many first editions by established Australian writers. The rooms smelt of an aesthetic antiquity that I found comforting and that attracted me. Whoever is or was responsible for those acquisitions has similar tastes to mine in the arts. This is the house, I remember, where my mother worked and where I played outside while she worked. Like the surrounding landscape, the cattle grid, the wheat, the sheep, the crows and galahs, this is where I identify with the "real" Australian countryside.

On my left, before I enter the driveway, is the split-slab hut with its louvered glass window high on the front of its V-shaped roof — the hut where I played under a corrugated iron roof, cobwebs, inside its walls lined with harnesses and ropes, among tables stacked with oil containers, funnels, cans, bags of concrete, pieces of machinery, tools and farming implements. A pair of metal scales hangs from one of the rafters. Peter will later inform me that the hut is the old Bartley's Creek shearing shed built in 1871 as a hay shed.

Outside stands a red combine harvester, a tractor, a fuel tank on a metal stand and several forty-four-gallon drums. There's the smell of dryness and dust that only a wooden hut like this can have. Gum trees grow to one side, huge trees whose bark is stripping. There's also the separate smell of diesel near the drums. Further back are shearers' huts that look like the small schools I once taught in. They've been joined together and create an elongated shape. There's a chimney at the front, its top crumbling, again an image out of Australia's past — perhaps the kind of dwelling that one of Henry Lawson's characters might have lived in, or Lawson himself.

Peter and his wife, Pixie, greet me at the door and formalities are exchanged. Peter explains and apologises that he couldn't be interviewed earlier in the week because of his involvement in the campaign for the National Party in the forthcoming state election.

I'm shown around the house and not long afterwards their son, Jason, joins us for lunch. At one point I remark about the guns on a rack on one of the walls. I describe the target practice that I witnessed down by the creek, past the tennis court, with the three boys on a day when my mother brought me with her to the property. I remember the pungent smell of gunpowder, turtle doves flapping in trees, the white tails of rabbits bobbing, escaping among tussocks. Before lunch, while walking around the property, we visit the tennis court that is now a brown sheet of hardened dirt, like a floorboard, a steel roller standing at one end, propped against the cyclone-wire netting, its perimeter fringed with bleached yellow grass. Among tall trees, not far away, is where the target practice took place. The sky's a pastel blue, light as shallow water, without a cloud in sight. Birds flit and sing among the trees; they sound like finches.

After lunch, Peter and I retire to the drawing room. He broaches the reason for my visit and says he doesn't mind being interviewed.

He begins speaking immediately and says it was one of the first times they'd used the circular saw. They didn't know much about it or how to use it properly. Andrew was on the handle of the machine. Peter's account is told in a quick voice: the cypress pine trees; the wind that blew back on the blade; the blade jamming and then becoming free, "coming out in a big arc"; Peter turning around and getting cut behind his knees. We talk a little longer and then he ends, almost abruptly, like a businessman or politician speaking.

I tell him how I discovered the incident as a news item on microfiche, but not in the newspapers because all the copies from 1951 were missing.

The topic of conversation changes to a strong memory I have: the name of the small black horse I'm sitting on in a photograph taken on the property. The same horse that threw me. Was it Pig?

Peter says the horse was called Dodger because he'd dodge his head around when anybody attempted to put a bridle on him. He was also called Pig because he became fat.

He shows me his collection of books. We speak about our favourite Australian poets and he proudly displays his collection of Will Ogilvie volumes, tells me that Ogilvie worked and lived in this area. We share our memories of who studied what for the Leaving Certificate examinations and discover our subjects and results are similar.

When it comes time to leave I give them the gift I brought and request a photograph, as I did with the other two brothers. They agree and stand before a climber rose, itself outlined against the dark green and pink of the homestead, Pixie in a pink blouse, Peter in a blue shirt, his arm around her. One is smiling, the other laughing, both so happy, like teenagers in the sunlight, green grass at their feet.

I feel no regret in driving away from the property. There's a lightness, a feeling of relief, in a sense, that all the interviews have been completed. What each brother said has helped me to understand the events of that day in May 1951. Whatever buried images the events have revealed, whatever disturbances they caused, subconsciously and consciously, perhaps now, with these explanations, they can be laid to rest in peace. I remember the headlines that I copied down in the library earlier in the week:

FRIGHTFUL INJURIES IN CIRCULAR SAW ACCIDENT
TWO LADS SUFFER SEVERE LACERATIONS

The memory prompts me to make a detour to the library before returning to the motel. To my surprise, I'm informed that the toner for the photocopier hasn't arrived yet from Bathurst. I remember promising Mrs Dziuba I'd return and take some photographs. Also, I have a gift for her, a small doll bought in one of the gift shops.

As I turn into Russell Street I can already see Mrs Dziuba in her garden, on the footpath in the centre, facing the street, her three Pomeranians snapping at the air, barking at the stranger who has returned briefly into their lives to say goodbye.

That evening I drive out to the Radio Telescope with Anthony Boys, a friend of my son. Anthony is working in the Forbes–Parkes area, selling calculators; earlier in the week we'd made contact and arranged to meet. Afterwards we eat in the restaurant at the Bushman's Motor Inn. It is good to have company from Sydney.

Trying to get to sleep under that vast central-western night sky, I imagine the souls of my mother and father somewhere among the galaxies of stars, moving on, among creation, bodies free of illness and pain, minds free of memories.

10 Mary Street

I am running down a dirt road of stones and gravel; long paspalum weeds grow on either side and they have black sticky ends so that the seeds attach themselves to skin and clothes. The dirt of the road has been packed hard by cars and the timber lorries that deliver logs to the three-ply factory in Bellona Avenue, just around the corner from where I live.

There are vacant blocks of land between the houses, land covered in paperbarks, wattles, blue gum and prickly scrub. On the western side of the street, behind our house and the five others, runs Duck Creek; it is full of bulrushes and wild fruit trees grow along its banks — peaches, lemons and sour oranges. Duck Creek was named after the brown ducks that fly up from the water; they quack loudly when you surprise them and they have emerald green, black and white in their plumage.

Between these houses and the creek is an uncleared tract of land, a council reserve, too narrow to be built on and which has never been cleared since we moved into the street. Blue-tongue and frill-necked lizards live there; so do black snakes. Blue cranes and kingfishers live along the creek, as do other birds that belong to Sydney's undeveloped suburbs — peewits, magpies, cranes, doves, sparrows, blue wrens, willy-wagtails, kookaburras, silver-eyes. Totally overgrown with trees, weeds, blackberry bushes and white moth plants, the area is our playground, our Garden of Eden. We build our cubbyhouses there, our bonfires. There we play chasing and hide-and-seek. Any game that we can think of that will take us away from our homes and into the freedom and camouflage that such an environment gives us. By "our" I mean the small gang of children that is running down the street with me — or, rather, of which I'm a part. We run as one. We are yelling, calling out, shooting capguns and arrows into the air. Some of us are cowboys, others are Indians, girls and boys alike, whooping in the afternoon sun that is pouring down the street and turning light into pure gold. We feel no heat, no thirst. We are never hungry except when it's time to go home, when our mothers call us from front gates or over backyard fences and we climb those fences and disappear through doors into kitchens and dining rooms.

Most of us are barefooted or wear sandals. The boys wear shorts and short-sleeve shirts. The girls wear summer cotton dresses. There are six of us, four boys and two girls. Sometimes there are more, depending on who joins us from neighbouring blocks, from Elaine Street, Carlingford, Clapham, Barbara or Helen. There are many streets in Regents Park with girls' names.

Nearly all of us are immigrant children. Some of our parents know each other from various Displaced Persons' camps in Germany or migrant hostels in New South Wales, or they met on the ship coming to Australia; others have become friends since moving into this suburb or into the street. Theirs is a close community and they socialise as often as they are able to, but many of these adults work double shifts in factories, shops, on the railways, or for the Water Board like my father does. They come home and then go out to work again at another location, often not too far away from home. Many are building their own homes on these blocks of land on weekends while they live in garages. This is happening all over Sydney, all over Australia. They have brought their building trades and skills with them and are putting them to excellent use. Others, like my parents, have bought a home and are working to save money so they can pay it off as quickly as possible. In the meantime they are making the house a home — painting it, furnishing it, creating vegetable and flower gardens. For all of them it will be a far cry from the lives they left behind as a consequence of displacement and dispossession. All this is being done for themselves and, in the long term, the sake of their children.

In the years to come I will hear my parents argue about the house, about the circumstances that led my father to put a deposit on it while he was working in Sydney and my mother and I were living in the camp in Parkes. She will blame him for not consulting her, claiming he should have waited and they could have chosen a house together. She makes the accusation that he was influenced by friends from Germany and Poland who had purchased homes in nearby suburbs. He, true to his nature, will say little by way of explanation. He will swear for a while and then go off to the garage or chookshed and smoke until the disagreement passes. He never explained why he chose Regents Park as a suburb, or that particular house, and it won't be until almost forty years later, when I visit Raciborow, his birthplace in Poland, that I will begin to understand why — not until I see the resemblance between his village, set low on a plain, surrounded by forests, with a railway line running through it, just like the railway line running through Regents Park. Mary Street, too, is set on the low side of the northern part of the Bankstown municipality that is prone to flooding from Duck Creek because of a poor drainage system reaching further back towards Birrong and Potts Hill Reservoir. The whole suburb is surrounded by trees, bushland and vegetative growth, with dirt roads running through it except for the two main sealed roads.

But a little boy of eight or nine doesn't know what he will learn as a grown man. First he must run like the devil with his own playmates and chase the wind until he is hoarse from yelling and laughing — running into somebody else's backyard to play or the whole gang of friends disappearing into the bush, to go trekking down to the far end of Duck Creek where they think they'll catch eels.

I am examining various official documents that belonged to my parents; these have been stored in large plastic wallets and kept in the drawers of one of the wardrobes in my father's bedroom. They are papers relating to the purchase of our home as well as my parents' wills.

We moved into 10 Mary Street, Regents Park, in November 1951, and the earliest photographs that exist of the house are three black-and-white ones taken in 1952. They are approximately 3 inches by 2 inches, so worn with age and handling that the print has started to wear off and all three are starting to turn brown. I have never discovered who took them. In each of them my parents and I are dressed in our best clothes.

Compared with what it became in the next four decades, the house appears old and almost dilapidated, and yet it was only five years old, having been built by one William Henry Joshua Hyde on land purchased from Mary O'Curry, widow, of Strathfield. The house was named "Shirleen". Alexander Allen Brown, a retired railway employee from Pyrmont, purchased it from Hyde and my parents in turn purchased it from him on 27 November 1951, as the Certificate of Title states, "at 57 mts. Pt 12 o'clock in the afternoon". The firm of solicitors acting in the sale and purchase of the property were Charles A. Morgan, Potts & Cullen of Somerset House, 9 Martin Place, Sydney, also at Parramatta. The purchase price was £2700, of which my father paid £270 as deposit. A loan of £1600 was arranged through Manchester Unity. Five pounds was added for a rates adjustment with a further £73 3s for fees. A month earlier, on 5 October 1951, one Leslie Joseph Hall, of Homer Street, Kingsgrove, surveyed the property which was then known as "Lot 12, No 9 Mary Street", Regents Park. The mortgage was discharged on 30 December 1955. My parents had paid off our home in four years!

The writing on another set of documents is in blue, in copperplate, the style I was taught in primary school. The papers are stamped in blue and purple ink and parts of them are underlined in red ink. Where there is typing, it has been done on a ribbon typewriter.

The CERTIFICATE OF NATURALIZATION AS AN AUSTRALIAN CITIZEN is a document that belonged to each of my parents, although my name is written only on the back of my mother's. I was told that because I was under sixteen years of age I was automatically included in the oath that my parents took. But why am I only on the back of my mother's papers? Was it because Feliks was not my biological father? Both are dated 15 July 1960 and signed by the then mayor of Bankstown, Murt O'Brien. The certificates are embossed with a portrait of Queen Elizabeth II.

Something begins to gall me, makes my skin grow prickly. I feel anger rising inside me. My breath shortens. I want to escape into my earliest memory, into the darkness, but cannot.

We are sitting in a spacious office, my parents and I. There is brown linoleum on the floor. The walls are painted in cream colours. The two desks are of a dark hardwood. Chairs are a grey metallic colour, as is the filing cabinet at the back of the office. The door at our backs is of the same hardwood as the desks and has a translucent glass panel. My mother is to my left, at a desk, away from us. A man is interviewing her.

On my right, my father is being interviewed by a young woman. She is dressed in a blue two-piece suit and has short blonde hair. We are being "processed" to determine our eligibility for Australian citizenship and I am acting as my father's interpreter. That he arrived in Australia in his mid-forties, has had little contact with those outside his ethnic work groups, and manages with only a rudimentary English vocabulary, is of no consequence to the interviewer.

He answers to his name, age, address, occupation, his birthplace and country of origin without difficulty, but he is becoming increasingly nervous and his body language betrays him. He crosses and recrosses his legs. His hands are starting to shake. He has become hesitant, unsure of himself.

The blonde's formal approach changes. What does she sense, what does she read into the situation that makes her smile secretly? She now starts to speak quickly, and that is my father's downfall. While she spoke slowly, and I translated, he kept pace with her questions, was able to compose his reply without assistance, but once the speed of questioning changed, became what I can only think of as an interrogation, then he became nervous, unsure of his answers.

She asks, Do you have any hobbies at home?

Hobbies? Is she serious? My father works all day in a pick-and-shovel job for the Water Board, leaves home early and returns late; then he's out in the garden, doing what he's been doing all his working life. The garden is his hobby. I know what his answer will be.

I translate her question. My father says to tell her that his garden and chooks are his hobby.

I begin to tell her and she stops me cold, holds up a finger. Uh-uh, she says and shakes her head. He must answer himself.

My father says, Yes, I have garden. I have chooks. There is nothing secretive about his smile. It is a smile of pure nerves, coupled with an anxiety to please, but he also wants to flee.

And do you have a rooster? She asks.

Kogut, I say to my father; then in English, Rooster.

Oh yes, yes, my father replies happily. He senses that he is making progress.

And when your rooster and hens breed, how many chickens would you have on an average hatching?

Breed. Average. Hatching.

What's she up to?

She looks up with her cold blue eyes straight into my father's and pow! She's got him. She's got me too. I might be able to translate that, but it's his answer that she wants, and she knows he's confused at the length of her question and its vocabulary. This is the start of a short but scary rollercoaster ride. I can feel it in my bones!

I translate and my father shakes his head, shrugs his shoulders.

What do you mean? Don't you know, sir? Can't you count? Look, it's easy. She holds up a hand, spreads her fingers and wriggles them in front of my father's face. His face has reddened and I know he won't answer. He turns away from her. As far as he's concerned, the interview is over. One, she says, two, three ... Look at me, sir ...

A mirror could not show me anything I don't already know about the colour of my face. Red and getting redder. Shame creeps over it, spreads like a port-wine birthmark.

I start to reply. I want to explain. I want to help my father. Again the blonde cuts me short. She says, He must answer himself. That's the rule. Now, we'll try again. How — many— chickens — do — you — get — when — your — rooster — and — hens — breed?

And what you have for breakfast last week? Tell me! My mother has whipped around from her interview and her voice cleaves the room's atmosphere like an axe. She fixes her eyes to the blonde's and will not release them until she has humiliated her. I know that tone of voice. I have seen that look many times. Well, can you not talk? she asks.

Madame, I am only doing my job.

No, you are making fun of my husband. That is not your job ... I work for professional people, business man and doctor in Strathfield. I see how people do job properly. Shame on you! She shakes her finger at the blonde.

The man who was interviewing my mother leans back in his

chair, hands behind his head. He winks at me. Smiles. My palms are wet, drenched in sweat.

He must answer the question, the woman says.

Must not must, my mother shoots back. She has stood up and approaches her. Must go to toilet when must.

Sit down, please.

He has one rooster and twelve chooks. Sometimes we have ten chickens, sometimes twenty. We have plenty fresh eggs. Would you like some?

No, thank you. I'd like you to sit down and mind your own business.

He is my business. My son is my business. You make fun of a good man who works hard because you think you are clever. Come to Poland when you are forty-four and see how quickly you learn language.

That's my mother's trump card, her parting bullet. She makes her point irrefutably. The blonde knows she doesn't have a legitimate answer. She says nothing but doesn't lower her eyes. There's a lump in her throat. She swallows hard.

Okay, says the man, that'll do. Thank you, Mr and Mrs Skrzynecki — he mispronounces the name — thank you very much for coming in. You, too, sonny, you did splendidly for your father. He stands up, smiles at me, comes over and pats me on the head. My, you're a fine boy ...

As long ago in time as that encounter was, it remained fresh in my mother's memory until the end of her life. We spoke about it, she never without bitterness at the mockery that was made of her husband — and my father — by someone she referred to as *a little bitch*.

There is nothing more to browse through among the papers in the two wallets, nothing that I haven't seen before, nothing that interests me at the moment.

The recollection of the incident with the interviewing woman reminds me of stories my parents told about the Displaced Persons' camps in Germany, stories of the numerous queues and interviews they were subjected to before having their application for emigration to Australia approved.

When they were moved around Germany by the Allies after the war, when they lived in transit — on trucks, buses, trains, a ship that was nothing more than a converted troop carrier — did my parents ever dream of the house and street they would move to one day?

I doubt that what I learnt in later years of Regents Park and its history would have been of great interest to them, though they would have listened to the facts. Despite its regal name there has never been anything high-class about Regents Park. It always was, and still is, a working-class suburb. The suburb's name originated from a property built by a Mr Peck and a Mr Jackson in 1897. They chose the name from that part of the north-west of London which had once been a favourite area of the Prince Regent, who was later to become George VI. Various subdivisions of land were made earlier in the 1800s and at first the suburb was called Sefton Park, but the arrival of the railway in 1914, to what is still a junction, connected Sefton and Chester Hill on the Liverpool side, and Birrong and Yagoona on the Bankstown side. In May 1929 the suburb finally became Regents Park.

Neither our family nor any of those arriving with us in the early 1950s were aware of our suburb's association with London or the Prince Regent. Nobody knew anything of local history. It was a suburb overgrown with bushland. However, it was well situated for transport, for buses to Auburn and Lidcombe, for trains to and from the city, to and from other suburbs where other homes were being built. There was work in factories, in warehouses, on the railways, in shops, for the Water Board. You could buy meat from a butcher called Jock in Amy Street, a big man with black curly hair who waved to all the kids who walked past his shop on the way to and from school. A baker from Lidcombe called with bread once a week, or it could be bought in one of the many corner shops. A milkman brought milk in a cart drawn by a Clydesdale. He would click his tongue and the horse would follow him up the street, stopping exactly outside the house where the milkman was. The toilet can was emptied by the "dunny man", who drove a "night cart" that smelt offensively when it was parked out in the street in summer. Land was cheap. Demand for manual labour was strong. Men, women and children bonded in an environment that was raw, unsophisticated, unsullied, that challenged their expectations of themselves and their future.

Regents Park became my home suburb until I moved away in 1967 to my first job, a teaching position in a one-teacher school at Jeogla in north-western New South Wales. Strangely, the names of streets have stayed with me, stayed alive, imprinted with an ink that all the rain fallen since 1967 hasn't been able to wash away.

The Streets of Regents Park

The streets of Regents Park
run in the same direction
that they did when I was a child —
when I played in them
and the suburb was a bushland
of wattles and paperbarks.

Amy Street still joins
the suburb, running from east to west.
On the Sefton side, where I lived,
Clapham Road joins Park
at the top of the pipeline bridge
and continues to Chester Hill.

Those were streets of dust and gravel
from where I got my bearings
no matter where I had to go —
school, play, swimming at Banky Baths,
the pictures at Lidcombe:
leading away but also bringing me home.

I belonged to a "gang" of children
who played alongside Duck Creek
and its paddocks of paspalum —
in those long golden summer afternoons
that were always never-ending.
We built bonfires that burnt past midnight.

Houses, shops, factories,
an influx of new immigrants
now lay claim to the streets —
witnesses to the lives of my parents
and the generations before them
who made the suburb what it is today.

The streets of Regents Park
still run through my blood
even though I don't live there anymore —
leaving was like walking into another room
and discovering, afterwards,
there was no lock on the door.

Eels

Let's go down to New Africa, says Leon. Let's explore.

Okay, says Stefan.

Yeah, says Ziggy.

The girls, Veronica and Rhonda, agree.

"New Africa" is our place of mystery, of discovery, set deep in the bushland, beyond our homes. We go there to spend time together even if we only search through rubbish that's been dumped along the banks of Duck Creek or we shoot arrows at a rabbit we might startle, or someone might even see a snake or a blue-tongue lizard that goes *aaahhh* when it tries to frighten us with its fat blue tongue.

Six little bodies run on twelve legs like those belonging to ferrets or corgis, short and swift, until they run out of breath and must slow down or stop, not caring who sees them or how far they've come from their homes. It's still daylight. Maybe it's the school holidays or maybe it's the weekend. Who remembers or cares? They are all caught up in the delirium of the moment, this special time together, when they are all brothers and sisters. Sometimes they quarrel and fight, they "gang up" in twos and threes, but in the end they will make up and share their lollies, their fish and chips, their chewing gum, their bottles of Pepsi or GI lime. In their own minds they know there is nothing they cannot do — even though they don't know the meaning of the word "heroes". They don't know whether they'll become carpenters, doctors, prostitutes, electricians, school teachers or receptionists. They haven't learnt about heart attacks that kill, about madness or the distress of broken marriages, about venereal disease or the ravages of alcohol on the body.

They point bows and arrows at one another. Those that don't have cap guns or pop guns cock their thumbs and point their forefingers, taking aim at each other.

You're dead!

No, I got you first. Bang! Bang!

Quick, get down. Here comes another arrow!

They slow down, breathless.

There's someone coming towards them.

Mrs Daphne Cutler and her horse. Her old nag Dolly.

Mrs Cutler lived directly across the road from us, with her husband, cranky Bill, and a boarder, kind, red-faced Charley White. Once I visited their house with my mother and saw that Charley's quarters were an old tin-and-fibro shed. Just one big room with a bed, a wardrobe, a dresser, a chair and a table. Between the shed and the house was the laundry. Further up the yard were chooks and geese and ducks. There was also an enclosure for Dolly. Like my father, Charley would "roll his own" and he told us he liked to be left alone. In Dolly's yard was an open shed with a tin roof. There, Mrs Cutler brought her food and water. People complained about the smell that came from the yard and the council promised it would be cleaned out; but as long as they lived there, nothing was ever done about it.

We were frightened of Mrs Cutler because she disliked us. Not just us but our parents and all migrants, even though there were more "New Australians" than "other Australians" living in Mary Street. She would wave angrily at us, call us names like *wogs* and *dagoes* and threaten us with extermination because we were stealing her country.

Stick together, says Ziggy.

Get out of her way, says Leon.

We know how much she loves that horse and would never let anything happen to her — even though grownups said Dolly should be put down. Dolly's eyes weep. Her hindquarters are scrawny and stick out like they are carved from wood. She walks with her head lowered. Her mane is matted with grass.

Get outta my way, you kids — go on, all of yers.

Get out of her way? What else could we do? We stood aside, watching her pass. It was as if Queen Elizabeth II had arrived in New Africa.

Mrs Cutler carries a bucket and shovel. We can see the horse manure in the bucket as she walks past.

Let's go down to Granville, Stefan calls out.

Or Parramatta.

Or Sydney Harbour.

But whenever we start our explorations, something always happens that stops us from reaching Granville and we never really go further than to the back of Auburn.

I reckon we might meet a bogeyman, Ziggy says.

A bogeyman wouldn't scare me, replies Stefan. I'd get my dog Blackie to bite him.

Your dog's not here, I say.

She'd come if I whistled.

Go on, taunts Veronica.

So Stefan whistles until he's blue in the face and saliva stops running out of his mouth. She must be asleep, he says. Don't matter. She'd bite him if she was here.

By now we are deep into New Africa, approaching one of the tunnels that lead into the tangled undergrowth.

It's like being in a Tarzan movie, says Ziggy.

That feeling of being in total darkness comes over me, that hint of the memory of first being alive. I am not scared but I start to feel nervous about going on. I slow down and drop back.

Hey, what's wrong with him? asks Leon.

Nothing, says Rhonda. She skips over and takes me by the hand. Follow me and you'll be safe. She's the only girl in our group who is not from a migrant background. She and her parents were already living in Mary Street when the rest of us moved in. Like another Australian family, the McAlpines who live in Clapham Road, the Brandy family has welcomed us.

I'm not scared, I say.

Then what's wrong? asks Leon. You're acting pretty strange.

Nothing! I call back. Disengaging myself from Rhonda's hand, I run on.

Ziggy sprints ahead and outdistances us all. I'll kill 'em! I'll save the world from all the mad people!

There's a light in the distance, small patches of sky shining through the tops of trees where their branches criss-cross like stitching on a blanket. Birdsongs are coming through more clearly, and that means we're getting to the end of the track. Ahead lies Duck Creek and the pipeline it flows under.

Where'll we go? asks Leon.

Straight ahead, says Stefan. Follow me.

We made it! Ziggy screams. Told you I'd kill all the enemies along the way. They were mad but I was madder! He leaps into the air and crosses his legs in a scissors motion, hitting the ground and falling over from the effort. We ignore him. Sometimes we tell him that he's mad because he thinks there are people in the world who want to hurt him. I have seen him under a table in his house and refusing to come out when his mother calls him. Nothing will coax him out of a hiding place and he cries and begs people to go away or he will kill them. We play and pretend when we are "killing baddies", but for Ziggy it is real. He swears that one day he will own a real gun and then no one will threaten him. I'll get them first, he says.

I wish I had an ice block, says Rhonda.

Me too, says Veronica.

The girls are very close friends. Veronica has dark brown

hair and says that one day she's going to marry Stefan and live in Hollywood where the film stars live. Rhonda has blonde hair and says she's going to marry a rich man and live in Kings Cross, wherever that is.

Ziggy blurts out, Let's go back. I'm going home.

I'm not going back, says Stefan.

Me neither, I say.

Me neither, says Leon.

I am, Veronica and Rhonda reply together.

See you all later, Ziggy says, lingering to see if anyone else will follow. When there is no response, he whips back to the track and disappears.

The two girls hesitate, look at each other, and follow him.

We've got ice blocks at home, Rhonda calls back.

And we've got cordial, calls Veronica.

Let them go, says Stefan.

Yeah, adds Leon. That Ziggy's always been a sissy.

Stefan, Leon and I walk slowly. Not much else is said because we're all thinking the same thing: should we go back or go further? And how far? The further the better, because later we can boast about our exploits, however small.

Gee, I'm thirsty, says Stefan.

Me too, I say.

We can drink creek water, says Leon. Like the Indians do.

You'll get sick, I say. There's taddies in there — and guppies. They live in that kind of slime.

Nah, says Leon. I'll go where the water's clean. He jumps down the creek bank and approaches a spot where there's a recess in the clay. Confidently, as if he's been doing it every day of his life, he bends down and scoops up water in cupped hands. See, it's clear. He throws back his head and drinks. As he does, he is screwing up his face, closing his mouth, and letting water run down his chin. Ah, that was good, he lies. You should both try it!

Bull! yells Stefan. You spat it out.

Did not!

Stefan and I climb down. We lie on our stomachs and splash water over our faces and necks, down our arms. Let's get into the shade, I suggest.

The day has become hotter. We glisten with sweat and creek water.

I wonder if Rhonda and Veronica are eating their ice blocks yet? asks Leon.

Who cares? I say, throwing a stone across the creek and watching it disappear into tall grass.

We continue lying in the shadow of a paperbark, a large tree whose roots have grown towards the edge of the creek bank and right through it; they are black and protrude like the gnarled limbs of a subterranean creature trying to break out from the earth. Some of the roots are thick, others thin, almost wispy. They are struggling towards water and light.

Above us, in the tree's crown, birds are fluttering turtledoves, with that unmistakable soft "coo". One, then another, flies off. I shield my eyes, trying to locate their platform nest of twigs.

There's a dove's nest, I say, pointing into the tree.

Let's find it and break the eggs, says Stefan.

Nah, says Leon, that's boring. We've done that before.

Why don't we fall asleep and when we wake up the world might have changed. Like Rip van Winkle did, I suggest.

That's stupid, says Stefan. Always the rational one, he sees no point in dreaming, in wasting time on illusions. Some day he might become a scientist or a doctor.

The three of us lie there, lost in the space of trees and water, bulrushes, cobwebs, hearing birds and insect sounds in the grasses and branches. We have no concept of time passing or purpose. We are neither grass nor stone, soil nor water, yet we might be existing as all of them, in a suspended state, in a kind of dream world.

What was that? Leon calls out. Sshh, listen!

We lie there, unmoving.

I can't hear anything, says Stefan.

That's a peewit, I say.

Not that, says Leon … Listen. In the creek.

From the creek comes a soft but rapid splashing sound, again, again. A sliding sound from out in the middle, where the water is deepest, and it's getting closer. It begins to rush backwards and forwards, then towards the bank, becoming lost among water cress and bulrushes.

What's that? I ask.

It's like a small submarine — look how it cuts through the water. Stefan points and we stare at the movement. There are several of these things rushing, whipping about, almost like a game's being played.

Eels! Leon calls out. This must be where the eels live.

Wow! we all exclaim.

We are fascinated by the sight of creek water being parted and bubbles being churned into foam.

I think they're playing a game, I say.

Nah, says Stefan. They're hunting for food.

Let's hunt them, says Leon. He whips out his shanghai and selects a large red ironstone from the edge of the creek bank. Watch this! he yells. *Plop.* He misses whatever he was aiming at because it makes no difference to the turmoil in the water. Again he tries. Again the stone plops, sinks. The eels continue thrashing the water.

Our eyes become accustomed to the glare on the water and it becomes easier to see them, to make out their thick olive-black backs and yellow undersides. There must be six or seven, sleek and shiny.

I'm going to catch one, says Leon.

Yeah, let's. Stefan is excited at the suggestion.

Let's, I agree.

Without thinking twice, without considering the consequences of what we're doing, or how deep the water might be, the three of us jump in fully clothed.

The bottom of the creek is soft, muddy. The water reaches our waist. Straightaway it has an "off" smell and tastes like there's something dead in it.

Yuck! I cry. Whose stupid idea was it to jump in?

You wanted to, says Stefan.

Who cares about a bit of stinking mud? asks Leon. I'm going to catch an eel. Watch an expert!

He takes a few steps forward, to the middle of the creek, and disappears under water.

Hell! Stefan is screaming.

Leon's drowned! I'm screaming. Help! Let's get help! What if he's dead already?

We know that none of us can swim. We're starting to panic. What can we do?

Bubbles are rising where Leon disappeared. Water is moving around, like an undercurrent is churning it. Like it's about to erupt.

Leon suddenly surfaces ahead of us, arms waving madly, half dog-paddling, half swimming, legs kicking. He is spitting water and mud, coughing, crying, but getting closer to the bank and scrambles up when he does. He clutches at clumps of weeds and just flops there, exhausted, breathing heavily.

We wade over to him, taking big strides, then we haul ourselves up next to him, trying not to upset him. He keeps his eyes closed tightly.

No one speaks. Leon is the strong one in our group. He can punch and wrestle like nobody else. To see him lying there on the grass — breathless, trying hard to stop crying, his sandals full of black mud that's running on to the grass — is an embarrassment that Stefan and I will never speak about to anyone else.

I look down at my ankles and scream as loudly as my lungs

will allow. At the same time I brush and scrape at my legs as if they are on fire.

What's wrong with you? Stefan yells.

Leeches! I scream.

Now we are all wiping our legs, arms, bodies. We've had experiences with these bloodsuckers before and they really are harmless, but they are horrible to look at — fat, bloated, almost round, like slugs, once they've feasted on your blood, before they drop off. The leeches that live in Duck Creek are black with brown stripes and brown underbellies. They attach themselves so you feel nothing; but finding them unexpectedly, like now, produces a fright.

The sun continues blazing down on our heads. The three of us smell like mud, and the bush buzzes with the sound of insects and birds whose life we have disturbed. Our shanghais and Stefan's bow lie beside us. Sparrows are hopping down the creek bank. The creek surface is still once more and there's no sign of the eels.

When I was underwater, says Leon, I caught hold of an eel. God, it was slippery.

Lucky you, says Stefan.

Lucky me? laughs Leon. I nearly drowned. What am I going to tell my parents?

Tell them you slipped into the water, says Stefan.

Yep, I say. Me too.

Okay, says Stefan. That's our plan. No one's going to know the truth.

Have the eels gone? asks Leon.

All gone, I say.

Weren't they great to watch? he asks.

Sure were, says Stefan.

We lie there, the mud hardening on our clothes and skin. We make small talk, but it is important because we have to make Leon feel good again. We have taken off our clothes and sandals and hung them on branches. We lie in the sun, oblivious to each other's nakedness.

Wanna go back? I ask when I feel the moment is right.

God, I stink, says Leon.

We all do, I say, but it doesn't matter. A bath will take care of that quick smart.

Okay, says Stefan, and jumps up. Let's hit the track.

But get dressed first, says Leon. We don't want to run into any girls.

Or old Ma Cutler, I say.

Wouldn't that give her a shock? asks Stefan. Seeing our dicks.

She'd die from shock, says Leon.

How about those eels? I say. Weren't they whoppers?

Always are, says Stefan, as if he'd been catching them all his life. The creek's full of them. You're lucky one didn't bite you on the bum.

We laugh like idiots. There's nothing in the world to worry about. Leon didn't drown. That's all that matters.

We continue laughing as we squeeze into clothes and sandals that aren't quite dry and we pocket our shanghais. Stefan shoulders his bow like a real Indian would.

Returning from New Africa we are the heroes, the explorers who have discovered the secret place of eels. This will be our brag for the week, or even the month, until we venture further into the bush next time.

The Holiday Outing

The knock on my door is gentle, not too loud, but I'm awake and responding already to its message by leaping out of bed and getting dressed hurriedly. It's half-past five!

Ready, Peter?

Coming, Dad!

Breakfast's ready.

Our rooster crows in the chookshed in the far corner of the backyard.

A magpie releases its liquid song somewhere in the bushes behind our house.

A dog barks.

Sparrows chirp in the gutters.

A train rumbles in the near distance on the line between Regents Park and Sefton.

When these sounds start to filter into the house I know that dawn is breaking.

The reading lamp on the desk next to my bed fills the room with an eerie half-light and creates enormous shadows. It's like being in the room with ghosts that are also giants, with heavy shoulders, huge backs; their heads are domed-shaped rocks, moving about, watching me.

My father is a punctual man, very strict in his sense of duty. There is a routine to be followed from the moment he gets up to the moment he steps out the front gate. If he is late getting to the railway station he will miss the train. If he misses the train he will miss the bus connection at the other end of the line; then he will be late for work. That is not an option, certainly not because of a ten-year-old child. Son or no son, he will not be late for work. He uses the expression *Moja służba*, which means "my duty" in Polish, when referring to his work. He regards work as a responsibility and duty, and nothing deters him from that attitude. He never uses "sickies" to miss work — and he never misses work.

In the kitchen my mother is preparing breakfast. Normally Dad prepares his own breakfast and is gone before Mum and I are up, but this outing was promised to me a long time ago, as a present for my birthday. I am on school holidays and must be on my best behaviour. I must not get in anybody's way, must do exactly as I'm told and not embarrass my father. That's the bargain. If I break the rules, I'll never be allowed on such an excursion again.

Eat well, says my mother. You can't travel on an empty stomach.

She has set out a bowl of two Weet-Bix, warm milk, bread and butter, salt, a bowl of sugar. Eggs are boiling in a saucepan on the stove.

My father is already eating, has half finished his meal. Before he goes to work each morning, he fills an old dented aluminium basin with water for the chooks in their enclosure and puts out their feed in wooden troughs that he's built; this includes wheat and "mash", a mixture of a bran-like substance and water. If there are greens, leftovers from the garden, like lettuce or cabbage leaves, he throws in those also. A small door at the bottom of one of the walls connects the chookhouse to the yard and he opens it. At night, when the hens and rooster return to their perches, the small door is closed.

My father returns from his outdoor chores and I'm finished and waiting, my coat buttoned. Before stepping out, I kiss my mother goodbye.

On the back steps, Bobby, my dog, is madly wagging his

tail. He must think he's being taken for a walk. He looks up into my eyes expectantly and I pat him, ruffle his coat and tell him I'll see him this afternoon.

For a long moment I shiver, remembering the warmth of the eiderdown and wishing I was back under it. This is only the end of autumn, the May holidays, but the weather is cold. The air is damp and attaches itself to my face. Warm air condenses. Small clouds of breath drift into the morning light and disappear. The spell of sleep has been broken and a different one cast. There's a scent of freshness in the garden that is a combination of fruit trees, vegetables and damp earth. I breathe it in, especially the scent of those trees closest to the house — lemon, mandarin, plum, apple. The deeper the breath I take, the more eager I become about setting out. It's like the garden is giving me extra strength. I hear sparrows at the back fence, near where the chooks are scratching in the soil of their enclosure. For some strange reason I think about people dying, but I push the thought out of my mind.

Morning is weaving its invisible scarves of light around two figures about to leave their home before the sun has broken through the clouds. They are two ghosts materialising with the shrouded morning light. The grass is wet and their shoes have left imprints on it.

My father kisses my mother goodbye and I hurry after him.

The walk to the railway is a brisk one: six or seven minutes and we're there, with minutes to spare before the "All Stations To Liverpool" comes rumbling in from Berala. There are other early-morning workers standing and waiting on both sides of the platform, mostly men, some smoking, some reading newspapers. My father and I don't say much. I watch as he positions us at a certain point along the platform, because, as he explains, This way we will be near the ticket barrier at Liverpool. That station will be busy.

The train, a suburban "red rattler" — so called because of its colour and the noisy way it shakes when in motion — arrives and we sit on the right-hand side of the carriage facing each other, mostly in silence, until my father takes out his pouch of Jubilee, a tobacco with which he rolls his own cigarettes. This is what it must be like when he's alone. Mum doesn't like him smoking; she says it's not good for his health and won't allow him to smoke in the house. The cigarette smoke affects her breathing badly. This morning it's different, however — this morning it's just the two of us; two men going off to work. He lights up and blows blue cigarette smoke into the air. He crosses his legs and asks, as if he's read my mind, Well, how do you feel about being a working man?

I'm not like you, Dad.

This will be good for you.

Why?

You'll see what happens after school — how people have to work to make a living. This is a different part of life from what you are used to seeing.

The sky is streaked with an overcast yellow. The sun is now rising slowly behind clouds as if does not want to emerge from behind a haze. Streetlights are still on. Houses have their blinds and curtains drawn.

The train is travelling along the south-western line, through Sefton, Chester Hill, Villawood, towards Cabramatta and Liverpool. From there we will catch a bus out to Green Valley where my father is part of a Water Board road gang putting in pipes for water and sewage in the suburbs being built on the outskirts of what is known as the Sydney Metropolitan Area. Apart from working on a dairy farm at Ingleburn when we first arrived in Australia, this is the only work my father has done. A working-class man, he has only known farming and manual labour all his adult life.

How much longer, Dad?

Warwick Farm is next, then Liverpool, then the bus for fifteen minutes.

I've watched him adjust his Akubra hat a few times and

each time he does it he looks at his reflection in the window. He is not a vain man but it seems to me that this part of his clothing is important to him. He also runs his hand over his face and rubs it, as if checking that he's shaved.

The roofs of suburban houses rush past us, red terracotta tiles on the mostly fibro cottages. The backyards of these fibro homes have an outside toilet or "dunny" and smoke rises from some chimneys. There are garages and sheds in the backyards, rusting shells of cars on blocks, the occasional set of children's swings, a sandpit, dogs chained to kennels, vegetable gardens where choko vines and convulvulus trail over fences and incinerators are made from forty-four-gallon drums.

A feeling of intense interest in my father comes over me between the last two railway stations. For a quick moment I look at him and feel like my mind is spinning backwards, like it's going into a deep funnel, through grey shades, until it's all black; but there's also a light in the darkness and that light is the knowledge of something very private, something I never speak about. This is the memory that I've lived with all my remembered life, the one I've never told anybody about, a memory of coming into the world. How can I say to anybody — or even my mother — that I remember being in the womb and what it was like being born? Or to my father, Feliks, who is not my biological father, that I have these glimpses of dark and light, of pressure and pain, of hearing a lot of crying and sobbing because my mother was by herself? Her crying was for a loneliness and pain I've never felt myself, and fear because the war had not ended at that stage and she was far from her home in the Ukraine; but it was a fear mixed with tears of joy, also, because she said that I was her own and nobody, *nobody*, would ever take me from her. She kept saying that over and over, all the time, even after the midwife arrived from across the valley and helped to "clean things up", as my mother told me. This was the midwife who incorrectly registered my birth date and brought it a day forward, thereby making me a day older.

I also remember two colours, yellow and green: a yellow like butter and a soft green like the leaves around a cob of corn. I associate these two colours with the room that I was born in. Once, when I mentioned this to my mother, she replied, No, that's impossible! You had no way of knowing that! She brushed aside the conversation and never again did I mention the colours to her. In 1989, when I visited Germany and made contact with the family that my mother worked for during the war, I was taken to her living quarters in the barracks behind the steel-products factory that the family owned. There I received one of the biggest surprises of my life. As Fritz the owner pushed back the two sliding doors to reveal my mother's quarters, there was the room that I was born in — and there were the walls, green and yellow, exactly as I'd remembered them. When I asked Fritz how long the walls had been like this, he replied that they hadn't been changed since the war and, as long as he lived, they would stay the same. They have memories for me, he said. He said nothing more and walked away from the conversation.

My father's face comes into focus slowly, the features emerging into the light of the railway carriage, as if in a blur, discoloured by a haze of blue cigarette smoke and sunlight. I want to lean across and hug him and kiss him, say thank you for being who you are, for looking after Mum and me all these years and I hope that I make you proud of me. I like "Skrzynecki" as a surname even though there are boys at school and kids in the streets who make fun of it. He smells of cigarette smoke and Sunlight soap. His hands are rough and calloused, strong from doing outdoor work with a pick and shovel.

Come on, says my father, we're here. Time to go.

My secret disappears into my mind and I hear my father's words like a soft bell. *Time to go.* We stand up and he ushers me ahead of him. Through the window I glimpse the cream-coloured letters of the words "Liverpool Station" painted on a green seat just before people stream past and block my view.

The Water Board site is a collection of machinery, a large crane, backhoes, compressors, pumps, jackhammers. Several tin sheds stand along one side and most of the men go in that direction. These are their quarters where they share their camaraderie, where they change into work clothes, where they wash and later dress for the return trip home. Around the rest of the perimeter there are steel and concrete pipes of different sizes stacked on top of one another, as are bags of cement. There are several mounds of blue metal and sand. Hoses run in all directions and water bubbles up from a pipe in the ground, forming puddles of creamy-brown sludge that looks like melted chocolate ice-cream with caramel topping. Picks and shovels stand against the sheds. The men who have changed into their work clothes wear overalls or old pants, old shirts, hats of different types. Most wear gumboots. Some speak in English — theirs are the nasal accents of the "dinkum Aussies", the "True Blue" citizens of the country. Others speak in their mother tongues. I recognise Polish voices, an Italian, a German, a Russian. There are also Hungarians, Czechs, Yugoslavs. These are the "New Australians", the imported manual labourers.

We are heading in the direction of one of the sheds when a man comes running over and shakes my hand. Welcome, welcome! he says enthusiastically. My father steps back, almost as if he expected this display of exuberance. Even before we are introduced I know who he is. My parents have spoken about him many times. This is Harry Hamilton, the immigrant from Hungary who arrived in Australia a few years before us, a man who married an Australian woman and anglicised his name. A man who wishes to become a success in Australia and likes to impress people with his command of English. He still speaks a broken kind of English, however, and accentuates his vowels to sound educated, but his Ss come out like Zs, and as a result he sounds neither European nor Australian. Your father iz very proud of you, he beams, yez? You are clever at learning.

Me, clever at learning? If he knew the number of thumps I've received at school and the names I've been called to describe what an idiot I am, he would not call me clever.

My father motions for us to move on towards the shed where he'll change into his work clothes, which are hanging on a peg in the corner. He and Harry Hamilton exchange words that I can't catch but there's an understanding between them that means it's all right for me to be here. There is a contrast between the two men that's impossible not to notice at the beginning of the day, becoming more apparent as the day goes on. My father, quiet and confident, older, seems sure of what he's doing. By contrast, Harry Hamilton is anxious and impatient, running around like a rabbit, trying to do ten jobs at once, trying to impress the workmen with his skills as a manager, his organisational ability, but really giving the impression that he's alone, that the men would know what to do whether he was there or not.

At ten o'clock it's time for "smoko", and the men stop for a cup of tea and a cigarette. An older man on the site, wearing a dirty white singlet, is called the Billy Boy, though the men also call him Jack, and it's his job to prepare the tea in a large, blackened enamel pot that's placed on a table near the sheds. The men wander in from all directions, from out of nearby bushland, people's backyards and further up the road. It's like watching ants appear from a hole in the ground. There seem to be more men than I saw this morning. They pick up cups and mugs of tea from the table. Sugar is in an old biscuit tin with a spoon stuck in it. There is no milk. My father brings me a cup of sweet black tea. He has poured himself one and we sit on two overturned clay pipes and drink. He asks me what I've been doing.

Walking around ... I even went down to the river.

Don't go too close to the edge. The grass is long and the soil is soft along there — even where the tracks are worn in. You could easily have an accident. A boy drowned not far from here.

I think of the times that Stefan, Leon, Ziggy and I have jumped into Duck Creek and waded across, sometimes with our clothes on, and never had an accident. My father seems to be reading my mind. He holds up a finger, in warning. This isn't Duck Creek, you know. This is the George's River and it's nothing like the creek. In some parts it's very deep.

There's so much bushland.

This is a new part of Sydney, but it won't be like this for much longer. It's being developed. The Housing Commission owns it and soon there'll be new homes for people. After we connect these mains for the water supply we're taking the sewer right through that way ... from Liverpool all the way down. He holds up his arm and points beyond the immediate rows of houses and way past the horizon, drawing an arc across the sky.

Why must the bushland be cleared?

People have to live somewhere. Work like this means that lots of people get jobs. That is important ... having work. Earning money. Homes. Factories. Someday this will be a big part of the city.

How long will it be before the houses are built?

Oh, he says, as he finishes his cup of tea, years and years to go. You'll be a man by then ... but it's happening and it will keep on happening. This part of Sydney won't always be farms. Come on, back to work.

He tosses his cigarette butt into a watery patch of ground and takes our cups back to the Billy Boy's table. I watch a peewit swoop down from the sky and start drinking from the water. It seems tame, ignoring me as my father walks away, but it shrieks a protest when I take a step towards it and flies off.

My father's warning has made a connection in my brain between danger and death. A boy drowned not far from here. How old was he? What was his name? Who discovered his body? If the river flows from one place to another, why won't the words flow out of my mind? Why is there a fear in my mind?

After smoko my father and several of the men have begun working at a new trench and I wander over to watch them from a distance. A machine has been digging and they've gone down into the earth, setting up planks to support the walls and prevent a cave-in. A concrete pipe has been fitted into a sling and a crane like a steel monster will lower it into a hole. The men will then join it to another pipe. It's a deep hole that's not wide but looks more like a tunnel and inclines into the earth at an angle the way a slippery-dip would.

Peering down into the excavation from where I stand in the background, the day rushes up to me in images.

I see myself eating a black-pudding sausage sandwich and washing it down with black tea.

Harry Hamilton is bossing his men around.

The river flows lazily past my eyes, its green surface wrinkled by an underwater current.

Cranes and peewits fly overhead, wheel and disappear into the peaceful distances of paperbarks and eucalypts.

I am throwing pieces of blue metal into the river from a pocketful that I've taken from the site earlier in the day.

Cows and horses are grazing on the opposite bank.

Suddenly, my reverie is broken by a rushing of men from every part of the site. Harry Hamilton's voice can be heard above the general commotion. Back, men! Back! He is yelling, pushing men out of the way, as he forces his way to the hole. Weaving, following him, I manage to squeeze through the circle of men. The concrete pipe has slipped out of its sling and fallen into the hole. Below it, with his back to us, a worker is trapped, crying out in pain, calling out that his leg is broken.

Help me! Help me! Ah, hurry! Hurry!

Men are looking to their boss for directives. Harry Hamilton just keeps repeating, Back, men! Give him more space! But I can see that his eyes betray him, and I can hear that he's panicking. He has no idea what to do. He holds out his arms and manages to restrain the men nearest to him, all except one who pushes him aside and leaps towards the mouth of the sloping tunnel, landing on his backside and disappearing in two or three seconds, his hat flying off, pebbles and clods of earth following him, along with the long-handled, snub-nosed shovel he'd been working with. My father!

Before I can even call out, Dad, don't! he's gone and a loud collective *Aahh!* from the rest of the men follows him. Like a skier racing downhill in the snow he has braced himself into a crouching position, arms tucked into his sides — and down, down he went, almost out of sight.

Good on you, Feliks!

Bravo!

Losing my fear and getting closer to the edge of the hole, I see enough to understand what he's doing, that he's using the shovel like a crowbar, trying to lever the pipe back, just enough for the trapped man to slide his leg out. It seems to require a superhuman effort — but there's a grunt from my father and a loud *Hooray!* from the men around me. He has shifted the pipe. Two other men have slid down into the hole to assist. Once more, Harry Hamilton seems bewildered, uncertain what he should be doing. Back, men! he continues ordering. Make room, make room! Let them come up … Stand back!

The man's leg was not broken, just bruised and skinned; one of the workers drove him to the hospital and Harry Hamilton suggested the men have the rest of the day off. My father shrugged his shoulders at the idea and asked, How can we get home? There is no earlier bus.

The injured man was an Italian and to the rest of his countrymen my father was a hero. He was bombarded with one *grazie* after another every time they came up and slapped him on the back or shook his hand. He shrugged it off but also laughed, smoked cigarettes with them and shared their camaraderie as if he was an Italian himself or they were Poles. Perhaps their common bond was Europe or the fact that they were immigrants and understood each other in a way that only immigrants can.

For the rest of the afternoon I didn't leave my father's side, and neither he nor Harry Hamilton complained. Those men that stayed behind went about their work, but the whole atmosphere had changed. On one hand, talk was all about the accident, on the other, there was a casualness about everyone's activities — and you could sense they were just stalling for time, waiting for half-past four to come around, then they'd be off to the bus stop.

When my father stripped off to the waist and prepared to wash himself, I asked, How did you know the man's leg wasn't broken?

I didn't, he replied. I had to act quickly in case it did get broken. Time was of the essence ... Get my towel ready, will you?

Okay, Dad.

He lathered his face, arms and chest with a bar of Sunlight soap and poured a basin of cold water over himself to wash off the suds. Then another. Ah, that's beautiful, beautiful. I could see he was enjoying the experience. When I handed him his towel he rubbed it over his skin until it became red. That'll keep me awake until I get home, hey, son? He referred to me as "son" at special moments, and I was always conscious of the word when he did. Forty years later, when he was dying, as I held him in my arms and thanked him for being a good father,

I remembered the sound of his voice saying "son". In that small room of his, a room stripped bare of all but the barest essentials, it was a powerful word, like a single-word prayer.

When we were in the train, I brought up the subject of the falling pipe again. He explained that there is always a certain amount of danger associated with the kind of work that he does. Men often get their arms and legs skinned and bruised, or cut, and sometimes an arm or a finger gets broken. There are lots of heavy pipes to be moved. Cave-ins happen. You must act quickly in all these cases. One day machines will do all the risky jobs and men won't have to go down into the trenches … Sure, it's still work, but there's no future in it for boys like you.

I wanted to ask why, but he only sighed deeply, rubbed his big calloused hands together and rolled a cigarette.

Unlike the morning train, this one was a lot more crowded with men and women returning from the factories. We turned our faces to the window and watched the suburbs slip past. Cigarette smoke curled in the ceiling above us, creating a harsher kind of haze in the strong light. The accident belonged to another part of the day, yet I couldn't stop thinking about it. We were returning home and I was with my father, that was all that mattered. I never thought that my father's work might be associated with danger, but the accident had put a different slant on that.

It wasn't until dinner time that I mentioned the accident to my mother. To my surprise, she didn't seem impressed by what my father had done. I know he's a saviour, she said. Why do you think I married him?

Mum, he's a hero. A pick-and-shovel hero!

Hero, hero … Do you know what the word means?

It's someone who takes risks and saves people, someone who does great things.

Well, why don't you be a hero and eat your dinner?

Mum, Dad saved a man's life. Do you know how dangerous his job is?

Not really, she said. They must have spoken about the accident when I wasn't there. Why else would she be reacting like she was? During this conversation between my mother and myself, my father ate hungrily and smiled, apparently content not to be taking part in it. So, are you happy with your birthday present? she asked.

Birthday present? Of course! How could I have forgotten? Oh, yes — thank you. It was the best I've ever had. There's something more that I want to say … but I can't think of what it is. It isn't to do with Feliks not being my biological father and the way I noticed him as the train was pulling into Liverpool Station. It isn't to do with him calling me "son" and what having "Skrzynecki" as a surname means to me. It's not about the word "hero" and it's not about my memory of being born or the green and yellow room. Whatever it is, it's right on the tip of my tongue.

I'm about to leave the table and my father looks up, says, Remember what I said, Peter. There's no future in it for you.

Good Morning, Sister, God Bless You

St Peter Chanel's, Berala, is situated on the top of a hill between Regent Street and Kingsland Road. Today, it no longer exists as such, and is known as Trinity College, a Catholic high school run by the Catholic Education Office. The school was named after the Marist French missionary priest Peter Chanel, who worked in the Pacific Islands mission of Futuna.

My parents enrolled me at St Peter Chanel's after we moved into 10 Mary Street, first and foremost because it offered a Roman Catholic education and adhered strictly to the teachings of the Holy Mother Church; it was also renowned for its discipline. Both of my parents were from traditional Catholic backgrounds where it was considered a sin to eat meat on Friday or to miss Mass on Sunday, and that a child went to Limbo if he or she died without being baptised.

For them, Heaven was for the believers, for those who died in the state of grace. Hell was for the pagans, for the sinners. You said the rosary, prayed to the Virgin Mary, the Sacred Heart, the angels and saints. The Pope was God's vicar on earth and he was always an Italian. He was faultless — infallible! What he said, you did. Catholics didn't marry non-Catholics or they'd be excommunicated. You kept the Ten Commandments. As kids, we were told that if you died in the state of mortal sin you went straight to Hell. Hell, where maggots feasted on your flesh and intestines, crawled out of your eye sockets and mouth. The hottest fires ever imagined burned in you and around you for eternity. That meant for ever and ever and ever. And we believed it all!

We also prayed for Mary MacKillop, the nun who founded the Order of the Sisters of St Joseph, the order that ran the parish school. The nuns who taught me were nearly all Irish. Sisters Anthony, Dymphna, Fiacre, Ligouri, Brendan, Austin, Anne. Of these, I remember Sister Austin as being the kindest and Sister Brendan as being the most ill-tempered, impatient and brutal when it came to administering corporal punishment. She was renowned for the academic success of her students in the Primary Final examinations, but she was also infamous for the punishment she dished out with a cane, ruler or her knuckles. You were always a *bold, brazen lad*, and when the back of her hand connected with your ear or head it did so in such a way that you felt the wedding ring she wore because she was a bride of Christ. In all my years of Catholic education, first at St Peter Chanel's and then at St Patrick's College, Strathfield, a Christian Brothers college my parents sent me to in 1956, there were only two teachers whom I thought were unnecessarily strict. Of these, Sister Brendan wins hands down.

Upon entering the classroom every morning, our first duty was to stand at attention and address the nun in charge with the greeting, Good morning, Sister, God bless you. We had to be dressed correctly in navy pants, dark blue shirt and woven black silk tie with double gold bars running horizontally, cut square at the bottom.

The nuns wore a habit of dark brown, a veil and a starched white bib that covered their chests and looked like plastic, running from shoulder to shoulder. The veil was kept in place with black hat pins. Their necks were covered with white cloth, as were their cheeks. A strip of white cloth ran across their foreheads; this might have been the lower half of a cap. We used to wonder if they had hair, if they had breasts like other women or were allowed to marry priests. Beneath the bib was a blue lattice-type pattern with the letter J stitched into the diamonds the strips formed. They used men's handkerchiefs and kept these tucked into the sleeves of their habits or in a side pocket beneath the bib. Below the bib they wore a big black leather belt from which a set of black rosary beads hung and, at an angle, tilted to the right, was a large black crucifix. They wore black sensible shoes that were always shiny.

Subjects taught were Religion, Arithmetic, Algebra, Geometry, English, Australian History, Irish History and Needlework. The nuns were strict disciplinarians, teachers who tolerated no nonsense in the classroom and administered corporal punishment if you misbehaved or appeared to be not doing your best at all times. If they harboured regret or sentimentality for treating you like they did, I saw no evidence of it.

By today's standards, class sizes were large — forty or fifty pupils to a room. The desks were long and wooden. On weekends, when the partitions were opened and the room was used for Mass, the tops were folded down and the same desks became pews. We sharpened pencils and filled ink wells, used blotting paper so our pages wouldn't get smudged, ruled our margins and lines in red pencil and wrote meticulously in copperplate.

In the top right-hand corner of each page we had to write AMDG, the letters of the Latin phrase *Ad Majorem Dei Gloriam*, meaning To the Greater Glory of God. In English, it also stood for All My Duties to God.

Stefan and I were in the same class. One day he called out across the room, Hey, everyone — I know what the letters really mean! They stand for Aunt Mary's Dead Goat! The class burst into an uproar. Sister Brendan's mouth twitched, she trembled, turned scarlet, and Stefan received six cuts of the cane across his hands and had to stand in the corner of the room for the rest of the day.

For all their strictness, imposition of discipline and administration of punishment, the nuns were never really able to control all of us. There were some, like Stefan and Donny, who refused outright to conform to their rules. But in most ways, the rest of us did what was expected of us. We came to school because we had to; some liked school, others didn't. Some liked going to Confession, to the sacraments, to Mass on Sundays and Holy Days of Obligation. Many didn't. There were those who literally trembled when one of the nuns recounted the punishment of the Fires of Hell.

Why does God love us, Sister? Mary Duffy asked in Religion.

Because we are sinners, Mary — and God's love is so boundless, so great that He gave us His only begotten Son ... Yes, His Son to die on the cross, so that we may be saved from eternal damnation.

Stefan would snicker to me under the desk, and whisper, Maybe Mary will become a nun?

Mary was every teacher's pet, their darling. She was also the prettiest girl in the school, with a cute upturned nose and golden hair that she wore in a pony-tail. Many of the boys in fourth and fifth class were in love with her and wanted to marry her even though she never returned any boy's attentions and was only interested in talking to Donny. He would laugh and say, She's in love with herself ... But I'll get her one day. Donny was a year or two older than I was, but because classes were often composite, with, say, fourth and fifth sitting on opposite sides of the classroom, it was possible to develop close friendships with others than just those in your immediate year. So I learnt things from Donny about school and girls. But whatever he meant by "getting her" was a mystery, and I never dared to ask him what he meant.

Donny was a carefree, happy-go-lucky boy who had black hair and sang like an angel. He was also an only child. He lived close to the school, on the Auburn side of the railway bridge, towards Park Road. Like other boys, he was *a bold, brazen lad*, but for reasons I never understood the nuns punished him a lot less. There were rumours about his poor home life and his parents' health, rumours also about his family returning to Scotland to live. Donny would throw his head back and laugh like he was drinking sunlight, Ha Ha! Go back where? He was always needed as a lead singer in the choir when we sang at Masses and concerts. I figured that the nuns didn't want to upset him too much because he might refuse to sing for them.

The Sisters received their meat from a butcher in Park Road, and at one point in my schooling at St Peter Chanel's — because I had a bicycle with a wire basket that I'd carry my school case in — I was asked to ride over and pick up their order. This was written down for me and I was given money to pay the butcher. Take your time, Sister Fiacre would say. Just come back safely with the order. A kind woman, she was short and plump.

The trip took longer than I expected and my legs hurt from all the uphill pedalling, but I was doing this for the nuns, for St Peter Chanel, for God and ultimately for the good of my soul. Thank you, Peter, Sister Fiacre would say when I returned, and she'd give me threepence. Threepence! Think of the lollies that I could buy on the way home from school … Clinkers, cobbers, freckles … So I became the official errand boy who was sent twice a week to the butcher's. Those orders that didn't fit into my basket would be stuffed inside my shirt and I would pedal back to school looking like I was pregnant.

My secret job of bike-riding to the butcher's during school time came to an end when I was caught in heavy rain — a downpour that soaked me so thoroughly my clothes weren't dry by the time I returned home. I sniffed, sneezed, coughed and ended up in bed, needing medication. When my parents got the truth from me, all the lollies in Heaven could not have placated my mother's anger.

Sister, what are you doing to my son?

Nothing at all, Mrs Kornelia. He's been helping us — grand lad that he is — and, in turn, he was praising God.

No more. He must never ride to shops any more. School is for learning. God know that. If you had a child, Sister, would you send him out in rain?

The rain came unexpectedly, dear woman. No one planned it.

Not even God?

I'm sure God has his reasons, if he did. We are sorry. It will not happen again.

Such was the scene at the door of the convent when my mother brought me back to school after I'd been away for several days. She literally marched me to the side entrance and demanded to be heard. It fell short of a commotion but I was never sent again to the butcher for meat.

The key lesson every day at school was Religion — Religion as specifically set out in the Green Catechism. Its official name was the *Catechism of Christian Doctrine*. The price was six-pence and it had been issued originally under the Imprimatur of N.T. Gilroy, Archbishop of Sydney on 8/9/'43. Nineteen forty-three! Two years before I was born. This little green book would have such a profound and lasting influence on my life — and it cost only sixpence! Five cents! What a small price to pay for learning whatever you needed to know that would get you into Heaven.

Salvation depended on us learning prayers for all occasions. The Sign of the Cross was first; then you had The Lord's Prayer and the Hail Mary, the Glory Be to the Father and The Apostle's Creed, Grace Before Meals and Grace After Meals. There was literally a prayer for every part of the day, including a Prayer for Our Holy Father the Pope. A picture showed His Holiness Pope Pius XII, bespectacled, a hand raised in bene-diction, looking youthful and uptight, his thin lips set, as if there was something he wanted to get off his chest but couldn't bring himself to say it. The prayer was prefaced with the instruction: To be recited in all Catholic schools each morning.

So we prayed, morning, noon and afternoon, for His Holiness, for St Peter Chanel, for the Sisters of St Joseph, for Father Donovan the Parish Priest and for the Faithful Departed. We were instructed to pray with special fervour on Feast Days, Holy Days of Obligation, Easter, Christmas, during Mass and Benediction, in preparation for Confession and during the Stations of the Cross.

If we failed to pray we were loaded with guilt and shame, repeatedly told stories of the lives of the saints, those "holy" men and women who prayed to die in the state of grace. They did, and now sat at God's right hand in Heaven. Those who didn't, the sinners, now repented for their lapses and languished in Limbo or, worse still, burned in Hell.

Our home lesson was often from the Green Catechism, and we were given parts of these lessons to be learnt by heart for the Religion class next day. Some of these questions and answers were simple and the reply straightforward. So, the Commandment "Thou shalt not kill" was easy to understand. So, too, the Fourth Commandment, "Honour thy father and thy mother". But the First Commandment, "I am the Lord thy God; thou shalt not have strange gods before Me", caused me considerable trouble.

In our street lived a Russian family who boarded in the back of the house of another family. They weren't there long before it became evident they were religious, and every Saturday, on their Sabbath, as they called it, they went off to their church. They dressed in their best clothes, suits and dresses; their son wore a tie and the older daughter wore pink ribbons in her hair, gloves and a hat like her mother. The children kept to themselves and attended a private school in Strathfield. Are you Catholics? I asked Misha, the son.

No, he replied blankly. We are Seventh Day Adventists.

That means they're Protestants, said Stefan.

It means we are the true believers, said Misha, unfazed by Stefan's sudden knowledge. We worship God on Saturdays.

Bad luck, said Stefan. That means you'll never get to go to the pictures on Saturday arvo.

We have Bible lessons at our church; then we draw pictures and colour them in.

What sort of pictures? I asked.

Pictures of God and animals.

What does your God look like? I asked.

Like God, replied Misha. He has a beard and lives in the clouds.

So does our God, I said triumphantly. He holds out his arms and protects the world and all the animals. Fixed in my mind was the picture I had of God from *The Junior Bible and Church History*, another book we had to read and learn from at St Peter Chanel's. In the first picture God was in the clouds, his arms outspread. There were trees, mountains, rocks and water below Him. Rays of sunlight were coming out from Him. He wore a shirt with long sleeves and a cape over His shoulders. In the next picture He was creating animals. Again He was in the clouds, surrounded by stars and the moon. Below Him were a tiger, a lion, an eagle, a flying goose, a sheep, a rabbit, two giraffes, a reindeer, a camel, a horse, an emu and a kangaroo. Out on the waters a whale was blowing spray from its spout. Can I go to your church? I asked.

I don't know. I'll have to ask my mother ... And you'll have to ask yours.

Misha stood there unblinking, like a statue, his square shoulders hunched forward, giving him a sad, defeated look, like he was about to cry or have one of those asthma attacks we'd heard he used to get but never saw him having.

My mother gave permission for me to attend Misha's church and I accompanied his family one Saturday. The church was in the city and looked more like an office than a church. The polished furniture was a bright brown colour and there was a set of large glass doors. People wore their best clothes and the minister was called a pastor; he also wore a suit and tie. He carried a Bible and didn't look anything like the priest at St Peter Chanel's.

Misha and I were separated from his parents and sister and put into a small group. We sat at the feet of a lady who talked to us about Adam and Eve's wickedness and God's curse on them. Had any of us done anything wicked? No, no, everyone shook their heads. It was just like being in class with Sister Brendan. Are any of you telling a lie? She was very polite but her eyes were cold and went straight through me. You will burn in Hell if you lie to God! God knows if you are telling a lie! She thumped her knee with a fist and everyone at her feet sat up like frightened puppies. Does anyone here want to burn in Hell? Again, everyone shook their heads. The class was getting more and more like one of Sister Brendan's. No? No sinners here today? Very good. The lady smiled and handed out small coloured pencils and pictures of animals for us to colour in. Mine was a rooster. There would be a prize for the best finished picture, one by a boy and one by a girl. This is what I came for and I made sure that my picture was going to be the best. I used brown, yellow, red and dark blue to colour my rooster like the one we had at home. The blue feathers had to look glossy like polished metal but they couldn't be black. The red feather must look like blood, the beak orange but not too dark.

Your rooster is really good, said Misha.

How do you know? I asked.

I just do. The teacher likes you because you paid attention, too.

The teacher's name was Miss Kim and she did give me the boy's prize. She congratulated me and said, Welcome to our church … Let's give Peter a clap, children. They clapped but only half-heartedly. The prize was a packet of the same short coloured pencils we'd been using. I could take my rooster home to show my parents.

Misha whispered, Now you are one of us.

What do you mean?

It means you can come to church every Sabbath with us.

But I want to go to Mass with my parents tomorrow.

Can't. You are a Seventh Day Adventist now.

No, I'm not. I'm a Roman Catholic.

You speak Polish at home. You must have been a Polish Catholic. Now you have become a Polish Seventh Day Adventist.

Miss Kim stopped us speaking by clapping her hands and announcing that Scripture was over. We could go out into the hall and have milk and biscuits. Now that was something different from going to a Catholic Mass. Here they gave me prizes and fed me Monte Carlo and Milk Arrowroot biscuits. The milk was strawberry-flavoured and I could take a biscuit to eat on the train going home. Wait till I tell my mother and father that I am now a Seventh Day Adventist and have to stop going to a Catholic school.

Misha and his family delivered me home and reported on my good behaviour. After they left I told my parents all about the day and showed them my rooster picture and the packet of coloured pencils I'd won. Now I belong to their religion, I announced. Now I'm not a Catholic anymore. My father patted me on the head, as if to say, yes, yes, of course, and went out into the garden; my mother ignored me and went on peeling potatoes at the sink. *O Matko Boska*, she whispered under her breath. O Mother of God.

Mum, they've got a great religion. You should go on the next Sabbath.

I'll go to Mass tomorrow and so will you.

I'm a Seventh Day Adventist now.

You're still a Catholic and always will be. Listening to a pretty lady talk about Adam and Eve and getting a few biscuits and a drink of pink milk doesn't make you a Seventh Day Adventist.

What makes me a Catholic?

You were baptised a Catholic and you'll die a Catholic. So will your father and so will I. That's the way it is and that's the way it will be. Remember that. Listen to your mother and do what she says and you'll end up on the right side of the street. Misha and his family have their religion, we have ours. *Koniec!* That meant, End or Finished; it also meant that she didn't want to talk about it anymore. If I pushed her any further about this I'd end up on the wrong side of the wooden spoon.

But on Monday, at school, when I tell Stefan, Leo, Ziggy and Veronica that I went to Misha's church they say that I'll go to Hell because I broke the First Commandment and the *Green Catechism* says on page thirty-four that it's sinful to take part in non-Catholic religious services. It is a sin against faith. Mary Duffy overhears the conversation and goes telling tales that I went to a Protestant service.

Is that true, Peter?

Yes, Sister Brendan, it is true.

Why?

Because I wanted to colour in pictures and then I won a prize and they gave me biscuits and milk ...

Before I can finish Sister Fiacre comes on to the veranda and asks, What's all this about, Sister Brendan?

Peter went to a Protestant church service, Sister.

Sister Fiacre's hand goes up to her mouth. Oh, she exclaims. My, my, what are we to make of all this? Does your mother know?

Yes, Sister, my mother does know. So does my father.

And they don't mind?

My mother prayed to the Virgin Mary about me and asked her for help. She said O *Matko Boska* and that means O Mother of God. I also tell Sister Fiacre about Miss Kim, the rooster, the biscuits and everything else — even getting the extra biscuit to eat in the train on the way home. Sister Fiacre watches me and smiles. She pats my head and presses me to her side and I think, Why can't Sister Brendan be nice like this. Mary Duffy is pulling faces at me behind the nuns' backs.

God understands all about roosters and coloured pencils. Of course Miss Kim was correct about Adam and Eve and God's curse. Yes, yes, we must not tell lies ... Did you go to Mass yesterday?

With my parents, Sister.

See, all's well then.

That night I ask my mother why I can't go to the Marist Brothers School in Parramatta like some of the other boys at St Peter Chanel's are going to do. She says, It's because you're not ready — besides, when you go it will be to the Christian Brothers College in Strathfield. But not for another year.

But I'm in Fourth Class.

You need to grow up more. Your father and I have decided another year at St Peter Chanel's will do you good. Besides, you can become an altar boy and that will make us even more proud of you!

An altar boy! The nun in charge of training the altar boys is Sister Brendan. No, Mum! No!

I've already spoken to the Sisters, and Sister Fiacre has given her permission. She is the boss.

It's Sister Brendan who decides who finally passes the tests for altar boys.

Maybe, but Sister Fiacre says your Spelling and English are very good and you learn new words easily. Latin shouldn't be a problem for you.

Words words, blah blah blah ... I'd rather be good at Arithmetic and not get yelled at in Sister Brendan's Arithmetic classes.

But the end of Fourth Class arrives and I get a prize for coming first in English. The prize is a book called *The Eight*

Days Feud by G. H. Tempany, and it's about a cricket quarrel in a posh English school. I've discovered that I'm good at writing compositions, also stories about horses, storms and holidays at the beach, even though I've never been to a beach in my life and I hate storms. I'm scared of horses since Dodger threw me one day on the farm in Parkes.

My parents are pleased with me when I get selected to be a candidate for the Altar Boys Class. But Sister Brendan is still my biggest worry at school. She never says a kind word when I get the daily Spelling List one hundred per cent correct — and she screams her head off when she comes in to take Arithmetic. All she does is talk about her Primary Final students and the results they get. My parents will be taking me away from St Peter Chanel's before Sixth Class so I don't really care about her Primary Finals.

I'm now in Sister Dymphna's class, Fifth, and that's a lot easier than being in Sister Brendan's. Sister Dymphna is a big woman, stern but friendly, and my mother says she's Second-in-Charge. My father explains that it's like being the foreman at work. I understand that, and it doesn't take me long to get on with this nun.

When I make a mistake with division sums or how many square feet there are in a square yard or how many yards there are in a chain, she doesn't get cross. She says, Never mind, it'll come to you one day. Sit down, and we'll try again later. When she speaks about chains in Arithmetic all I can do is think about the chain that our dog's tied to and I have absolutely no idea why chains should be a part of Arithmetic.

The class is different now because some of the boys have gone away to Brothers Schools and Mary Duffy has been sent to a boarding school in the Hunter Valley, wherever that is, but it makes me happy. I hope it's far away. When I hear the words *hunter* and *valley* I think of jungles and natives and animals. Maybe she's lost and getting stung by mosquitoes and eaten by leeches and wild animals.

At home I boast about my new teacher and I'm told that I'm lucky to have Sister Dymphna. She is popular with all parents and nuns. My mother still does the washing and ironing for the nuns at the convent on Saturday mornings and she notices how they behave around one another. She says they pray a lot, they sing hymns in the convent chapel and they sit in the yard and sew and knit; sometimes one of them plays a piano. Sister Anne is very homesick for Ireland and cries. My mother says she understands her and they talk about their homelands. My mother cries too. Sister Austin is another nun who is friendly. These nuns have all responded to the call of their vocations, as we are often told in class, just like Father Donovan, the Parish Priest, and Father Doherty, the Assistant Priest. God has given the nuns talents — even Sister Brendan, to whom I now go twice a week after school and on Saturday mornings for Latin classes. My parents are filled with pride at my becoming an altar boy. My father says, You'll look like a Polish soldier in your altar clothes. It'll be your uniform.

Why will I look like a Polish soldier?

Because the colours of Poland are red and white.

Why?

Red stands for all the blood that people have shed in fighting for Poland. White stands for God.

I want to tell my father that I hope Sister Brendan likes soldiers who can't do sums but can speak in Latin. My mother says, Hush … All that talk about soldiers and blood in front of a young boy … Just be patient and wait until I go into Pellegrini's in George Street and buy your altar clothes.

She bought the altar clothes and I was able to get through serving at Mass without any problems; but altar boys also served at Benediction, a devotion practised by the Catholic Church in order to give adoration to the Blessed Sacrament, and that's where I ran into trouble. During Benediction, incense is burnt in a thurible, a brass vessel with a lid that's opened and closed by a chain that the server pulls up, while at the same time the thurible is swung backwards and forwards in a kind of rhythm — one, two, three, swing out. One, two, three, swing in. A piece of hot charcoal is placed into it. Powdered incense is then sprinkled on to the charcoal and pungent fumes are given off. The fumes become thicker as the charcoal burns brighter when the lid is raised and air is let in. The incense is a dried resin and its aroma is so strong that, to the unaccustomed or sensitive nose, the results can be disastrous. It made me sneeze whenever I got a whiff of it. My eyes watered. I couldn't see properly and, consequently, I mistimed the swing of the thurible more than once. Either that, or I would fail to pull up the lid in time to allow more air to come in and the charcoal would smoulder and extinguish. I'd accidentally bump the priest with it, or one of the other altar boys.

That's it, Peter, that's enough, Father Donovan finally ordered. You can stay home for the next Benediction … You're a poor little sneezin' fella, that's what you are. Sure now, with that nose of yours.

That's enough, Sister Brendan echoed in the sacristy afterwards. You've humiliated me again — and Father — and yourself. No more Benediction for you. Mass will do … Now stop your snivelling and dry your eyes. We're lucky you didn't set Father on fire now — the way you hit him with the flames rising from the thurible.

When a group of us were caught singing a "sacrilegious" version of *Tantum Ergo* during Benediction we were threatened with excommunication itself. In a low-keyed tone, Terence Murphy, who liked to clown around in the sacristy before and after Mass and Benediction, would start:

Tantum Ergo — Makes your hair grow,
Sacramentum — Makes you handsome.
Veneremur — Makes it stay more …

and we would follow slowly, hesitatingly, though it'd happened before that Terence got us into trouble but escaped punishment himself. This time, Gregory Hogan was with us.

Heathens! Sister Brendan bellowed. *Amadans!* The shame of it! And in the sacristy, in God's own house, within sight of the Dear Lord on the cross above the altar. Himself, hanging there for your sins while you blaspheme. Out, out with you! None of you deserve to be called Catholics. Go, go, and never darken this doorstep again!

Playing with Stefan and Leon in the bushes behind the house afterwards, I told them what had happened. She's threatened to expel us.

You're lucky, mate, Stefan replied. I wish she'd expel me.

Then you'd end up in a public school, said Leon.

And go to Hell, I said.

Nah, my Mum and Dad reckon that's all bull. All of a sudden he sounded wise, very grown-up, like he knew what he was talking about.

How come? My curiosity was aroused.

My Mum reckons that it doesn't matter what school you go to if you want to get to Heaven. Or even if you don't go to school at all. The nuns only tell us that to frighten us.

Don't worry about what she said in the sacristy, said Leon. She'll take you back. She needs you because you've got a bike and can come up in the mornings to serve at Mass … You're like a relative to her.

From Ireland, said Stefan, where they talk funny and pray all the time and believe in St Patrick driving all the snakes into the sea. I even heard that St Patrick didn't come from Ireland.

Who cares where he came from, I said. But there are no snakes there, my mother told me. She works for a doctor whose ancestors came from Ireland and he told her. So it must be true.

I reckon that's baloney, said Leon. Why would anyone want to drown a bunch of snakes? They eat rats and mice and things like that. They're good for nature.

You'd drop dead if you saw one, I said.

Bet'cha I wouldn't, said Leon. I wouldn't be scared of a black snake. I'd jump on it and break its back. I'd grab it by the neck and snap it with a flick of my wrist like this ... See! And he demonstrated just how to kill a black snake with a flick of his wrist. The way Tarzan does.

Leon put his hands up to his mouth, threw back his head and made a Tarzan call above the heads of paperbarks and gum trees, just as if he'd been in an African jungle surrounded by vines and tropical plants and was announcing to all the animals that he was King of the Apes or that he'd just killed a lion with his bare hands or a crocodile by ripping its jaws apart under water and drowning it. Suddenly, as if it was expected of us, Stefan and I did the same. Three Tarzans, yelling at the top of their voices. Each one's cry became shorter and more hoarse the longer they tried to outdo each other. They beat their chests and ran their fingers through non-existent long hair. They all knew the picture on the tube of Tarzan's Grip where a long-haired Tarzan is sitting on the back of a lion, forcing its head back, ripping its jaws apart, its open claws useless against the strength of Tarzan. The three boy Tarzans knew this picture and three of them tried to imitate it.

Now the talk of Ireland, school and getting expelled from St Peter Chanel's is forgotten. There are trees to be climbed, birds to be frightened, a creek to be crossed. As we tear off across Jensen Oval to a large gum tree where we know a peewit's nest has eggs in it, a devil-may-care attitude comes over me and I no longer care about being scared of a teacher. I only wish that Terence Murphy and Gregory Hogan were here to play with us. I run as fast as I can, catch up with Stefan and Leon, and the three of us race in line, charging through paspalums and into the afternoon light. We are laughing like we've heard something funny. I wish that Donny could be here also, even though he doesn't belong to the gang that lives in Mary Street — but we could make him a blood brother like they do in the movies when cowboys and indians cut their wrists and put them together so that the blood mixes. Donny can really laugh when he wants to and it'd be great to hear him right now as we're running through the grass into the sun that's burning so hard I think it will burn us up, but it doesn't matter because we are so happy and I don't care if we all just disappear into the light.

Next day, Terence, Gregory and I are called up before Father Donovan and made to apologise by Sister Brendan for blaspheming in God's house. She marches us through the playground and up to the presbytery door.

Father Donovan seems taken aback and asks, Who is it, who is it — what? He is shielding his eyes and sounds confused. He is wearing black trousers, white braces, a singlet and no shoes. He has red hair on his arms and chest, and on his head it's very thick. His nose has a sharp edge and looks like it could cut through wood. He must have been asleep.

Sister explains why she is here and we're about to say sorry, although Terence doesn't look in the least sorry and I think he's going to burst out laughing at any moment. He keeps turning his head to the side as if he doesn't want Sister or Father to see his face.

Now, the three of you, apologise.

The three of us say "sorry" in unison but Terence is still trying hard to keep a straight face. He is playing the fool and hoping to get out of trouble again.

I am sorry, Father — that I am, that I am, he says. He is trying to sound Irish by speaking like that instead of just saying "I am".

Father pats Terence on the head and says, Now, now, Sister, let's not be too harsh on the lads. He comes forward and puts an arm on each of our shoulders. Off you go, back to your classes. Father Donovan is scratching his head, yawning, probably wondering what he's done to deserve this interruption to his morning.

Thank you, Father, we call out. Turning on our heels, we run, each trying to outpace the other.

Sister Brendan is speechless, I can see it in her face. As we draw away from her, Terence calls out, See, it works every time!

Father Cornelius Donovan, BA, was born in Araglin, County Waterford, and ordained at All Hallows', Dublin. He was appointed Parish Priest of Berala in 1938. He replaced Father Maurice Carmody who had retired because of ill-health. This tall man with a deep voice, red hair, broad shoulders and a nose like an eagle's would remain as Parish Priest until 1975. During my years at the school — which was originally called Blessed Peter Chanel's — he was the One Who Ran the Parish in Every Respect, whether it had to do with the Parents' and Friends' Association, the Holy Name Society, the Legion of Mary, the Sacred Heart Sodality or the St Vincent de Paul Society. He was the leader of the parish, the social organiser, the accountant, the arbitrator. Even after I'd left the school, I would hear stories about the continued growth of St Peter Chanel's and it was all because of Father Donovan. He'd become a legend in his own time.

He was the one to whom I made my First Confession and from whom I received my First Holy Communion on 25 May 1952. My certificate shows a painting of Jesus giving a communion host to a small boy who has his hands joined and is kneeling on a cushion at an altar inside a church that has red and white marble pillars and floors, as well as a red carpet. There are lilies and small flowers that appear to be roses in the foreground and background, and a lit candle. Rays of light are beaming from an invisible source, illuminating the space between Jesus and the little boy. An angel is kneeling close to the side of Jesus and is holding a ciborium. The angel has no shoes. The printing below the picture says, "Remembrance of First Holy Communion at Bl. Peter Chanel's Church, Berala". My surname has been misspelt, with the "y" left out. The certificate is signed by Rev. C. Donovan in blue ink in copperplate.

Today, the Rev. C. Donovan lies buried in Rookwood Cemetery, near the Chapel of St Michael the Archangel, in the lawn section reserved for priests, under large brushbox trees, surrounded by a hawthorn hedge. Over the years, my mother would recount a conversation she once had with Father Donovan about their names — his being Cornelius, hers being Kornelia. Just like the encounter with the woman interviewing my father before we became Australian citizens, this memory concerning Father Donovan bothered her. Apparently he insisted that his name was the "true name", whatever he meant by that or whatever she thought he might have meant. There was a similarity, he agreed, but his was the true Catholic version. After all, wasn't it mentioned in the Mass, in the Invocation of the Saints? So what's wrong with her name? Well, he insisted, it wasn't a "true" name. He said that he was a man and that the Lord himself chose a man's form to live in upon the earth. He would point to himself, vigorously tapping his chest to emphasise the point. This absurd logic wasn't lost on my mother who, though not a trained theologian, was no fool either. Was he saying that because God chose a man's form, a masculine version of a name was a truer form? Not necessarily so, Father, she told him. God also chose a woman's body to carry Him and give Him birth. Wouldn't that make a woman, whatever her name, just as important as a man, if not more so? Maybe not, Mrs Kornelia, he replied. Who else could carry a child? Anyway, it's up to the Lord, who did choose a man's body, after all, to make Himself known to the world ... And so it went on. His was the "true" name and therefore must be the better — or more important — name. Was he also implying that because God chose a man's form to make himself known on earth, men must be somehow more important than women?

As the number of Polish immigrants in the western suburbs of Sydney grew, the arrival and influence of Polish priests became established in suburbs like Bankstown, Ashfield, Cabra-matta and Blacktown. Slowly, but evidently, the number attending Polish Mass grew. Priests of the Order of Jesus lived in Bankstown but travelled to these other suburbs to celebrate Mass.

These services were held in the parish church of the particu-lar suburb every Sunday at a specially allocated time. Most of the time my parents chose to go to the midday Mass at the Church of St Felix of Valois, in Bankstown, at the intersection of Chapel Road and the Hume Highway, opposite the Three Swallows Hotel. These Masses were solemn, grand occasions, with as much social panoply attached to them as to their reli-gious significance. Everyone, men, women, children, were dressed in their best clothes. Hymns were numerous. The ser-mon always included a plea to the *rodaki* — the compatriots, the countrymen and countrywomen — who were present never to forget the burden under which those living in Poland still laboured. This referred to the Communist regime that oc-cupied Poland after World War II. Prayers were offered to God and to Our Lady of Częstochowa, the Black Madonna, for the liberation of Poland. I used to watch my father's face and the faces of other Polish men and women at such times and saw how transfixed they were as the priest's voice rose in tone and how emotional they became as the priest denounced the Communists — as he exhorted people to pray, pray, pray, never to forget what an evil this Communism is and how it had enslaved a freedom-loving people, virtually making them pris-oners in their own homeland. The White Eagle on the Polish flag had its crown removed by the Communists because it symbolised the monarchy. Let us pray that one day the crown will be restored, the priest would plea — not because the mon-archy will be returned, but because when that day is born, that will be the day that Communism dies. Democracy will rule in Poland. It was like listening and watching a call to arms, a cry to rally in prayers and hymns. After the Mass we would walk to the railway station and often travel to whichever family's home we'd been invited to for lunch. If it was at Bankstown or a nearby suburb, we would walk; if it was in another suburb, we would walk to the railway station and travel by train, then walk.

These were happy times, always special, and times when all the mothers went to extraordinary lengths with cooking and food preparations, as well as showing off new chenille bedspreads, lace curtains, chandeliers and Axminster carpets that had been acquired since the last visit. Children played outside, becoming friends and hopefully starting to fulfill their parents' dreams of growing up in Australia to a far better life than their parents had left behind in Europe. Once when I chased Irene Budzinski through the rose bushes at 10 Mary Street, she tore her First Communion dress. Years afterwards, I learnt that she managed to get home and hang it up in her wardrobe without her mother noticing. Fathers smoked, drank spirits and poured beer from brown bottles. They reminisced about life in Poland or the Ukraine or Russia, or wherever their origins lay. Sometimes they became drunk and were noisy. Sometimes one would fall asleep and be left lying in one of the bedrooms, allowed to sleep before going home. Among others, we visited the Budzinski family in Brunker Road, Yagoona, the Truchnowskis in Bankstown and the Glicza family in Lidcombe.

When the long day finished, often well into darkness, our long trek home would begin, back through the suburb and its streets that led to the railway station, then sitting in semi-darkness, the waiting room lit by a single light globe, waiting for the train. We'd travel through the dark suburbs, changing trains at Lidcombe or going straight through to Regents Park, get off and walk up those planks of wooden steps, turn right at the top of the overpass, walk across Park Road, and then left, past a handful of shops where the owners eked out a living, over the pipeline bridge and down Clapham Road, turn right

into Mary Street and open the gate at Number 10 — my
mother and I waiting, listening, in the darkness while my father opened the back door, and then hearing the plastic "click"
of the switch as the light was turned on in the kitchen and
squinting in the brightness. In our home. Finally. Tired, foot-
sore, but strangely pleased.

Sunday Visits

1
We visited friends on Sundays after Mass
in Lidcombe, Bankstown or Doonside —
one of those western suburbs of the 1950s
where migrants like us had settled.

We travelled by train, then on foot,
from railway barrier to squeaky front gate:
the trio walking like a model family
dressed in best clothes because it was Sunday.

Met at the front door we were treated like royalty
to a sumptuous meal prepared beforehand
with other guests who had arrived for the day.

2
Children played in backyard vegetable gardens
while parents sat around dining tables
and talked of Europe and their exiles —
cursing Hitler, Stalin and how "the war years"
had forced them to emigrate to Australia.

Clouds of blue cigarette smoke filled the house.
Vodka and beer filled glasses and stomachs
as toasts were raised to absent friends, relatives —
or the "little ones" running around outside
in their discovery of the New World.

Oblivious to most of it we were climbing trees,
searching through neighbouring creeks
and uncleared bushland settings like pioneers —
setting dogs onto chooks and imaginary foes
who lurked in tall grasses, behind work sheds.

Girls played with dolls, prams, teddy bears.
Boys showed off on 24-inch bikes or scooters.
If anyone hurt anybody else you had to apologise
or be prepared to suffer the consequences
from one of the adults when they came outside.

3
Going home in the chill evenings, saying goodnight
at the front gate among the scent of roses,
the sound of a piano accordion or violin music
trailed in the air with its poignant European melody.

Worn out by the end of the day we were glad
to be on our way — though we smelt of sticky
paspalum weeds and the dust from the road on our shoes.

We knew nothing about politics, the causes of war,
and our "homelands" were now in the suburbs.
The lights of the railway station shone in the distance
like the altar candles at Mass each Sunday morning.

It was 1955 and my last year at St Peter Chanel's. For better or for worse, time seemed to be passing very quickly. That year my birthday fell on Easter Sunday and Sister Ligouri gave me a holy picture of St Aloysius. This was St Aloysius Gonzaga who, I learnt from my Daily Missal, was a Confessor priest, and was hailed as a "veritable angel in the flesh" because of his purity of life. At the age of nine years he had taken a vow of virginity, and entered the Jesuit Order at the age of sixteen. By 1591, at the age of twenty-three, he was dead, and Pope Benedict XIII proclaimed him "Patron of Youth". The image depicts him as a teenager dressed in a black soutane and white surplice. His hair is combed neatly. He looks impeccably clean, as if his body and clothes have been to the dry cleaners. He is holding a crucifix before his face, close to his lips. Beneath him, tall white lilies are growing out of the air, their flowers touching the hem of his robes. St Aloysius is praying, oblivious to human existence. He seems to be in an otherworldly place. Oddly enough, he resembled Father Doherty, the young Assistant Parish Priest my mother always thought should have married and had children.

Don't you think this is a beautiful holy picture? my mother asked, holding it up to my father. She was using the word "holy" a lot that night. She and I were sitting at the kitchen table when he walked into the house. I wonder why Sister Ligouri chose this one to give to Peter?

Maybe she wants him to be a priest? my father asks seriously.

Oh, do you think so? A priest? I've sometimes thought about having my son become a priest. Can you imagine receiving Holy Communion from the hands of your son? A mother would feel so special. So, so holy! Holy!

No, I can't, said my father. What about Confession? Telling your sins to your own son? Hey, Peter the priest, what penance would you give your mother?

Not me, Dad. If the nuns want us to be priests they shouldn't go around belting us like they do.

I agree, said my father.

Well, said my mother, you'll be at a new school next year — and the Brothers will educate you to be a Christian gentleman.

Your mother means they'll straighten you out with a strap instead of a cane if you play up, my father said.

Silly, silly, my mother replied, and waved away the conversation. Now, show me that lovely holy picture again, will you?

Here you are, Mum.

My, my, doesn't St Aloysius look holy ... You can see the light of God in his eyes.

They're closed, Mum.

Driving past the Regents Park Hotel today, and reading "Las Vegas Gaming Lounge" painted across its front, I find myself remembering — and thinking how ironic — that Father Donovan, a Confessor, lived there, "at the pub", as it was said, for twelve years before a new presbytery was built for him in 1952 in the grounds of St Peter Chanel's.

A new church, Mr McLean, he was reported to have said to the publican. We must now build a new church, a church that will be big and full of light, for I dislike churches that are small and dark and damp, such as I remember from the old country. The new church will stand on top of the hill in Kingsland Road and be seen from such places as Villawood and Bankstown — and even, Mr McLean, for sure, from Araglin itself.

So in 1955 a collection was begun for the building of this grand house of worship. We, as pupils at the school, were encouraged to bring in four shillings and sixpence each to buy a brick. Even though I wouldn't be at the school after 1955, my parents donated the money and were among the first group of parents whose names were read out by Father Donovan at Sunday Mass. To the Glory of God, Father Donovan stressed, holding up his hand as if he were proposing a toast — and all it will cost is fifty-two thousand pounds! God deserves nothing less than the best and the best we will provide! Parishioners coming after you will be in your prayers and debt forever more. Your love of God, your generosity and ability to work hard will be remembered in decades to come! Think of God, think of St Peter Chanel and think of your own immortal souls!

To the Glory of God, the congregation might have thought and agreed, but almost murmured, No, No, to fifty-two thousand pounds! Instead, they nodded their heads, remembering that the old building they were sitting in was a church-school and God did demand their loyalty. They were being led into the battle of fundraising by the greatest warrior-general who ever trod the polished floorboards of any Catholic altar and surely he wouldn't lead them into defeat. Then there was the matter of their immortal souls. Nobody wanted to burn in Hell. Many wore their brown scapulars that guaranteed dying in the state of grace; others were wearing their green scapulars, which meant they would not get sick. Good health, dying in the state of grace and contributing to the building of a grand church to the Glory of God. What Catholic man, woman or child could ask for more?

Cracker Night

We stand to attention like little soldiers in the playground during assembly while Sister Dymphna announces that next week, on the twenty-fourth of May, there will be a school holiday to celebrate Empire Day. She reminds us that all the pink countries on the world maps in our classrooms belong to Great Britain. Australia is not a colony anymore, but is still part of the British Commonwealth of Nations.

Who cares, I think to myself, as long as it's a day off school. I catch Stefan's eye and know that he's thinking the same thing. So are Ziggy and Leon. We'd like to give three cheers for the holiday but are forbidden to speak during assembly. Never mind, our thoughts are already in the bushland behind our homes. Next week, fireworks will explode there. There might even be a fire and the Fire Brigade will be called. The night air will become filled with smoke and the smell of gunpowder as double bungers, jumping jacks, sky rockets, sparklers and other kinds of fireworks explode, burn, blaze, fizz and shower in the name of a celebration we don't fully understand. Dogs will bark, hide in kennels and under houses; cats will disappear for the night or be locked up in their owners' homes.

The four of us usually made our bonfires separately, but this year we decided to work together and create one big bonfire. We called it "The Biggest Bonfire Ever". Bigger than a Hollywood production, as one neighbour in the street remarked when we boasted about it.

There were two secrets to making a bonfire that wasn't just a cone of branches and twigs that would burn itself out quickly. The first was to fill the centre with materials that take a long time to burn — car tyres were the best. The second was to build a big, heavy structure that resembles a haystack. First you built a tepee shape and filled it with tyres, crates, plastics, anything that would burn. Then, working from the outside, you built it up from base to apex with bracken, going as high as you can. In the end, your bonfire's shape was more of a giant rectangular prism, the top slightly peaked, like a mountain.

Why're we doing this? Leon asked. We know we can build bonfires. It's a cinch.

Because we want to build the biggest bonfire ever, says Stefan, and become famous.

Ah, that's bull, says Ziggy.

And we can't blow up any more letterboxes or tie bungers to dogs' tails, I say. Remember how the kids in Elaine Street copped it when their dog jumped off the railway bridge and got run over by a train?

Apart from letterboxes and dogs' tails, another trick of ours was to drop fireworks from one of the railings on either side of the bridge in Mary Street, below which Duck Creek ran. This required perfect timing and skill in lighting the bunger. First of all, because you were dropping the bunger and not throwing it away, you had to be careful and get the angle between the wick and match right, otherwise you burnt your fingers. Once you lit the bunger and watched the wick burn down, you dropped it just in time so that it exploded as it hit the water. We called these "water bombs". Let go too soon and the bunger didn't go off — it plopped into the water and you wasted a good bunger. Let go too late and you risked getting your fingers burnt or blown off. If it exploded in mid-air, in the mouth of the tunnel, that wasn't too bad — at least you heard an explosion that sounded like something in the movies. The side-effect was that it left a ringing in your ears that lasted for days and your parents thought you'd become deaf.

Every year since moving into Mary Street, I'd buy my fireworks at the local papershop and build my own bonfire while the others built theirs. On the big night we'd watch one burn, then another, another and another. Our faces became reddened from the heat of burning wood and smudged with soot and ash. Our clothes got dirty. That didn't matter. As long as we had a good time. That did matter. Next morning, the air still heavy with the smell of fires and gunpowder, we'd sift through the cold ashes and search for "fizzers". It took a long time for the image of glowing faces to recede from our memories and disappear into the nights of advancing winter. The sound of barking dogs faded and screaming cats disappeared over grey paling fences.

There was a boy in our neighbourhood whom we never insulted, whom we avoided if we could. He lived in Elaine Street and came from a poor family. He was already in high school, probably in Second or Third Year. His mother had a speech defect and his father limped noticeably, as if one leg was shorter than the other. There were rumours that his parents once worked as circus acrobats and that he had a "mad" brother in an asylum, whatever that meant. The family lived in a Housing Commission cottage and the grass in front of their home looked like it had never been cut.

His name was Neville Johnson, but his nickname was Rocky and this probably referred to the fact that he was so solid he resembled a walking rock — or maybe because those who'd been hit by him said it was like getting hit by a rock.

If he met one of us on the way to school he'd ask, Hey, kid, wat'cha got for lunch?

Sardines in tomato sauce, I'd say.

Nah, that wog food's rubbish. Why doesn't your old lady give you some devon? Hey, wanna wag school today?

No.

Don't be scared of them teachers. They're all sissies ... Got any money?

If I was walking with Leon, Ziggy or Stefan, or one of the girls, he'd leave quickly, otherwise he'd trail behind, flexing his muscles, sounding tough, proposing we go down to the canal for a smoke. Or, if I waited, he'd sneak into the papershop and "pinch some fags".

No, I'm not wagging. My parents would kill me and I'd get caned at school, too.

The cane don't hurt much. You gotta be tough, kid. Otherwise you'll grow up a sissy too.

The Foleys were a dark-skinned family who lived not far from the Johnsons. Maurice was the only boy among seven or eight girls. He was tall, thin, weedy, and walked as if his backbone was collapsing. His mop of black greasy hair was combed back in a wave. His clothes were bright, flashy, often a yellow or red shirt that contrasted with his black trousers. He wore boots with high heels like cowboys did. He giggled a lot and trotted after Rocky like a lamb after its mother. Rocky's name for him was "Doris". C'mon, Doris, you'd hear Rocky calling. Catch up, you little sheila!

Coming, Rocky, right away ... and off he'd run on his spindly legs, his praying-mantis shape contrasting with Rocky's solid frame. Rocky seemed to tolerate him, as if he didn't like him but still needed him. They both truanted, and stole from shops, especially cigarettes from the papershop or corner milk bar beside Regents Park station.

Empire Day itself was an anticlimax for our group. We'd built the biggest bonfire on the block and there was nothing left to do. After school and on weekends we'd worked with axes and tomahawks like social insects assigned to a task by our instincts.

Gee, it is big, sighed Leon, when it was finished. We all stood back, our hands, arms and legs covered in scratches.

Wow, I said.

Yeah, said Ziggy.

Told you we'd make the biggest! Stefan yelled in triumph, punching the air. He ran and threw himself into it. See, it'll hold!

Hey, be careful! Leon screamed. You want to knock down all our hard work?

Nah, never, he replied. This is so strong.

Stefan was right. Being a combined effort, it represented more than just another bonfire. The frames held because we'd worked the base of each pole into a hole dug before we positioned them. Several tyres were first placed down the centre pole, which was tied with coils of wire at the top. The space between wood and rubber was stuffed with any kind of debris that would burn. Lastly, the interior and exterior were padded with as many branches and bushes as we could lean against the whole structure. We even put bricks into the centre, stacked around each pole. So when Stefan threw himself against the bonfire it didn't budge. Maybe if Leon had done so it would have been a different matter.

Try it, Stefan urged Leon. Go on, see if it holds your weight.

Don't you dare! screamed Ziggy. You're too heavy. If you knock it over you'll be the enemy. I'll have to strangle you like this! He jumped into the air, put his hands around an invisible throat and, by the time he landed on his feet, the non-existent person was dead. See, that's how it's done. Buzz off, he threatened Leon again. But Leon just ignored him and walked away.

See you all on Cracker Night, he said.

Leon knew that when Ziggy became agitated like that, it was best to leave him alone. When Ziggy felt threatened, you backed off, showed him you meant no harm. Soon he would calm down, the bright red colour would drain from his face and he'd laugh a quivering, nervous laugh, stare at you with his big blue eyes and you'd be left wondering, *What was all that about?*

By the time Empire Day arrived, the bonfire was a week old and sufficiently dried out to burn quickly. From the back steps of my home I could see its peak rising among the treetops. Tonight would be special. Not even the excitement of New Year's Eve or Christmas Day could match it — though Christmas Day meant presents, and that was a different kind of excitement.

My parents had gone to work and let me sleep in. Breakfast had been left on the table for me, and after I'd eaten it I got dressed and headed off for Duck Creek and our bonfire.

No one else was there. I wandered along the back fences and creek. Where were the others? Surely one of them might have come down earlier? Maybe they'd gone down to New Africa?

I felt an urgency rising in me. Time. The warm weather. Trees. Everything was crowding me — even the sky seemed to be pressing down.

Without realising it, I'd blundered and lost my way. That kind of thing happened rarely in this part of our suburb, but I'd walked too far and now had to cross Duck Creek at an unfamiliar spot. Never mind, I quickly doubled back to where I knew we'd built one of our crude bridges. Getting lost was no big deal anymore. We'd placed a plank at one of the narrowest parts of the creek. I hurried across it, clambered up the side and heaved myself on to the bank that skirted the fence running across Jensen Oval. The paspalum was tall and thick.

In several places there were openings in the fence; palings had been torn away because it made entry to the park easier and you could watch a game of cricket or footy for free. As I passed these openings I glanced in without expecting to see anyone — but at the fifth or sixth opening my blood froze. I couldn't move!

In front of me, in the tall grass, were two bodies, Rocky and

Maurice! Both had their trousers down around their ankles. They looked like they were wrestling or fighting, one on top of the other, puffing and grunting.

I was too scared to move away. My heart was beating like a sledge hammer. Rocky must have heard it because he turned his head towards me and I spun around.

You little rat! Quick, get 'im, Doris!

I don't know why I had to run but I knew that I did — I had to run faster than ever before in my life. Rocky would pulverise me if he caught me. The whole incident happened so quickly, so unexpectedly, it was like part of a dream — except that this dream had turned into a horrible nightmare. I was dumbfounded. Struck by fear. Fear of Rocky was making me run.

Reaching the creek, I didn't bother with finding a bridge. I jumped in and leaped through the water. One. Two. Three. Water. Bulrushes. Weeds. I finally waded through it all and scrambled up the bank. The voices were still in pursuit, yelling, threatening, gaining on me.

I'll kill yer if yer tell! Rocky was screaming, over and over. Wait and see!

Wait and see! Maurice echoed.

Only our back fence separated me from danger. I leapt at it, one leg up, with my hands grabbing the top simultaneously. Pulling myself up and over, I fell and landed, full force, on both knees. God! That hurt! Maybe I'd broken my kneecaps? Even my jaw shuddered from the impact. Bobby was barking around me, acting like a protector. That was good. The noise would help to keep Rocky and Maurice away.

I ran inside, slammed the door, locked it. Bobby was barking, growling, sensing there was danger outside. Now I couldn't hear anything except the dog's barking and my own deep, grating breathing as I gasped for air. I needed water. My heart was still thudding. Boom. Boom. Pounding in rhythm with my blood.

Quieting Bobby, I stood at the kitchen sink and gulped water. I splashed my face and arms with it, then dabbed my throbbing knees with a wet washer. Flopping on to the kitchen mat, I waited, waited, regaining my breath and senses.

The kitchen sink was beneath a window that overlooked our back yard, our fence and the bushland beyond; it was the same view as from the back steps where I'd stood earlier in the day and proudly viewed our bonfire rising majestically among the trees. But as I looked out, my pride was replaced by despair when I saw that the best bonfire in the world was smoking — thick curls and loops of smoke disentangled themselves from dry branches and leaves, rose in a long yellow-and-grey column that turned into flames. Tongues of fire began to leap out from the sides, orange-coloured tongues that were becoming knives and swords slashing the sky, destroying all our hard work, all our effort.

Who? Why?

The dog followed as I ran screaming outside, protesting, Put it out! Put it out! even though I couldn't see anybody else there, until, in the distance, running towards the middle of Jensen Oval, I spotted Rocky and Maurice, laughing their heads off, pointing back to the fire.

Revenge! This was their way of punishing me for what I'd stumbled across. But why, what had I seen? I wasn't even sure anymore.

I climbed back over the fence and, without thinking twice, broke off a wattle-tree branch and started beating and swearing, trying to do the impossible, trying to save what was left to save. Stefan appeared, screaming as he ran over, Hey, what'd you do that for?

You dope, I didn't do it. Help me! Come on, hurry up!

Help? It's impossible, can't you see? We'll never put it out. He broke off a branch from a nearby tree and began attacking the burning heap — but it was impossible. No sooner would we extinguish one part than another would start burning. Our eyes were watering from the smoke. Hey, let's get our crackers and have some fun! Stefan suggested.

No way, I said. I'll let mine off somewhere else tonight.

Suit yourself, he said. That's probably a better idea.

We stood back, defeated. The fire gave a roaring *whoosh* as a gust of wind blew through it. It was a pity that Leon and Ziggy weren't here to see how their bonfire was burning. It was a wonder that more kids or even grown-ups didn't turn up to ask why a bonfire was burning this early on Empire Day.

Stefan asked, How do you think it got started?

I've got no idea, I lied.

We smelt of smoke and ashes. Our skin and clothes were blackened, dirty, and we looked like a pair of chimney sweeps by the time we were ready to leave the remains of our bonfire. The awful smell of burning rubber lasted long after the last branches collapsed into heaps of ash. When Ziggy and Leon came around in the afternoon we went to have a look. The stink of burning rubber lingered. Ashes still glowed. Smoke trailed in wisps like the tails of kites. We agreed it was terrible to find your bonfire destroyed. Down in the dumps — that's where our feelings were. We'd been reduced to bags of misery. Worst of all was not knowing how the fire started.

But what had I seen?

Rocky had threatened to kill me if I told what I saw — and I didn't want to die.

Weeks later, on a cold June morning, I met Rocky on the way to school, along the track that ran beside the pipeline. He walked straight up to me like he owned the world and asked me, Didja tell anyone?

I shook my head, feeling one hundred per cent scared stiff.

Good. If yer smart you'll keep yer gob shut. If you don't, then we'll burn yer house down. Okay?

I nodded.

With that he knocked my school case from my hand, hit me

over the head, connecting with my ear, and walked off, flexing his muscles like he always did to emphasise his strength.

My ear burnt as I thought about Cracker Night and what just happened. I resumed walking along the track and sparrows hopped beside me, twittered, flew up on to the pipeline and back again. Why was Rocky so worried? That I might tell? What I'd seen had become something of a blur. It didn't mean anything to me that I understood or could explain. If he hadn't burnt down our bonfire I might not even have remembered it.

Two Boys Fighting

I am in the office of the Headmaster, Brother J. Magee, at St Patrick's College, Strathfield. The room is more like a parlour than an actual office but it does have a desk and chairs. There is paperwork on the desk. It is the last school term of 1955 and my mother has brought me along to be enrolled for the following year. Brother Magee is a tall man with black hair and a big smile. He looks a happy man, a man pleased with his calling in life, as my father would say.

We have a reference from Dr John O'Brien for whom my mother has been working in Strathfield since 1952. He sent his sons here until secondary school, after which they attended Riverview College in Hunters Hill. We also have all my reports from St Peter Chanel's, but I've noticed that the letter from Doctor O'Brien is what Brother Magee is most interested in.

The building we're in is on the corner of two streets and set well back from the footpath, opposite the secondary school building where a statue of Our Lady stands, on top, with arms outstretched. Two large pine trees grow between the monastery and the brick fence. Roses blaze in the sun like red, yellow and pink fires. The air around them glows with a light that is unique, that is created only around roses and brightens the immediate area, making it seem that the roses are burning. I know this from the roses we have in our own garden. When I'm at home, it actually hurts my eyes to look straight into the faces of roses in full sunlight, into their centres where bees circle and buzz. Their perfume is fragrant, strong, so heavy I can almost taste it.

My mother has taken a fancy to the roses and has been saying, Aren't they beautiful? Isn't this a beautiful school? A college, Peter. You must be on your best behaviour at all times. The Brothers have an excellent gardener. Have you ever seen more magnificent roses, Peter?

Yours, Mum.

Other boys and their parents are also waiting outside on the lawns, sitting on benches in the sun. Some of the mothers wear gloves and hats; the fathers are dressed in suits. Nearly all of the boys are wearing uniforms from the different convent schools they attend. I'm wearing a white shirt because my mother always makes me wear a white shirt when I go to church and on other special occasions. Anything to do with church or priests is always a special occasion. Now, anything to do with Christian Brothers will be the same; but my school tie gives me away and I notice that it's the same as most of the other boys — that navy woven silk with gold bars and cut straight across the bottom.

Two of the boys are pushing each other around. I can hear them through the open door. Brother Magee is ignoring the noise, which keeps getting louder. Their mothers shake them by the arms and the two boys glare at each other like they're about to break out in a fight.

So, Mrs Skrzynecki, Brother Magee says in parting, as he escorts us from the parlour. We are happy to have Peter at St Patrick's College next year. Dr O'Brien is a good man, a pillar of the Strathfield community. He shakes our hands and pats me on the back. Peter will be looked after here. We give our boys the best education. We train them in the Spirit of Our Lord, Jesus Christ, to be ambassadors for Our Blessed Lady, and to be Christian gentlemen. He points to the statue of Our Lady.

As he says the words "Christian gentlemen" there is a loud noise, like a roar, and the two boys that were pushing each other around fall to the ground.

My gang's going to be called Robin Hood. Yours — yours can be the Sheriff of Nottingham, says the boy with straight brown hair that was slicked back but has now fallen across his face. He's laughing into the face of the other boy, the one with blond hair — and that's making this second boy even madder.

The Sheriff of Nottingham was the Black Prince — and — I — don't — want to be the Black Prince! I — I — want to be Robin Hood! The second boy is almost screaming. He has freckles, a solid build. He is slightly chubby. His hair is shorter and combed straight back, not as long as the other's. I can see that both are strong. Their hands are pushing into each other's faces and chests, but there's also anger in their eyes. This is not a sudden flare-up. This has been building. These two must know each other. Maybe they're mates? They are getting redder and redder in the face and both think they have a point to prove. Each one wants to win. Their mothers are calling out for them to stop this fighting, but the boys ignore them. Other parents are watching, hands held up to their mouths in shock. Their sons, who will become new pupils at St Patrick's next year, are laughing, trying hard to hide their enjoyment. In the tumble of wresting of bodies, before Brother Magee can come out and separate them, the blond boy straddles the brown-haired boy and pins his shoulders to the ground with his knees. He yanks his tie up and down very hard, very quickly. Using both hands now, he positions the knot and pulls the tie tight, into the other's Adam's apple. The brown-haired boy coughs, splutters, throws his arms around as if he's drowning. Now, tell me, Charley Kiggins, the blond boy screams, Who's going to be the Black Prince? He is defiant, ignoring everybody who is telling him to get off Charley Kiggins, to let him go or he'll be expelled before he's even enrolled. I don't care! he is calling back. I'm not going to be the Black Prince! He steals from people — and I'd never do that!

Somehow, even though his face is turning purple and his eyes are rolling, though he's given up the fight to try and heave the blond boy off his chest, Charley Kiggins manages to scream back, Never, I'll never give in!

Say it — say you'll be the Black Prince!

Never, Charley manages to answer back, but his voice is a strangled whisper, like the last drops of water running down a drain. His face is changing colour, from red to purple to blue, and back to red. His eyes are closed. Is he dead, dying, or just pretending?

Oh, Mother of God! He's killing him! My mother turns me round. Don't look!

Let me watch, Mum! This is a great fight!

Brother Magee is pushing through the circle of parents and pupils. He appraises the situation in the blink of an eye. He whips his cincture aside, puts his hand into his habit and pulls out a penknife. Opening it as he steps forward, he lifts the blond boy up by the shoulders, heaves him out of the way, kneels beside Charley Kiggins and cuts through his tie, sawing more than cutting because the silk will not part easily.

There, there, son, you'll be right as rain in no time. He leaps up, briskly adjusts his clothes and stares at the blond-haired boy.

And what might your name be, son?

Anthony Tully.

Anthony Tully, Sir. Brother Magee stares at the boy. He sounds stern but friendly at the same time. I like this man already. I want to see how he will dispense justice. Will it be like Sister Brendan, with a clout to the head, or a prod in the back with his knuckles?

What school are you from, Anthony?

Holy Innocents Croydon, Sir.

Turning to Charley Kiggins, who by this stage has regained

his feet but is still coughing and rubbing his eyes, he asks, What school are you from, son?

Holy Innocents Croydon, Sir.

And what is your name?

Charles Kiggins, Sir. The poor boy is rubbing his neck.

Ah, says Brother Magee, both of you are from Holy Innocents. What a coincidence. How is my friend, the school principal, Mother Brendan, boys?

They look at each other, surprised, but don't answer. What can they say?

Mother Brendan? Is he joking? Does that mean there's another nun in Sydney with the same name as the one that has tormented me for the last four years? I almost blurt out, I know a Sister Brendan, Sir, but manage to keep my mouth shut. Besides, I also want to see how this incident will turn out. Brother Magee continues ... And who might your class teacher be, boys?

The two reply as one, Sister Mary Lawrence, Sir.

Ah, Sister Lawrence, Sanctity personified! Boys, boys, or should I say men, men — for that is what you are now: men, men of God. How would Sister Mary Lawrence feel if she witnessed your behaviour just now? Would she be proud of you? Look, look into the faces of your mothers — those walking saints — are they proud? Or are they ashamed of the behaviour of their sons? And, men, what will your fathers say when this is reported to them?

By now Anthony and Charles are standing with hang-dog expressions on their faces, and both look like they're about to start crying. Neither one is game to look up.

All right, men, says Brother Magee, let's see you shake hands and apologise to each other.

Reluctantly, as if there's a gun pointed in their direction, they murmur, Sorry, Charley, and Sorry, Tony, and shake hands.

Now, says our new principal, I'll see you both outside my

office in a few minutes. Goodbye, again, Mrs Skrzynecki. Goodbye, Peter. Give my regards to Doctor O'Brien and his good wife, Molly ... and to all the O'Briens.

He waves to us and my mother turns me around, but not before she says, You have beautiful roses, Brother.

That's the fruit of the labour of a former principal — and gardener — Brother Quirke. He established those treasures. May God bless the man and may God bless you, Mrs Skrzynecki.

The fires of the roses continue burning, consuming the sunlight and giving up their own light and heat. My mother and I walk back to the corner, to the bus stop across the road where we will catch the 414 bus to take us back to Strathfield railway station. Wasn't that great, Mum — that fight? Do you think Brother will give them the cane?

Here, the boys receive the strap.

Strap? What sort of strap?

Oh, just a little strap that doesn't hurt much. You get it across the hand if you are naughty.

How do you know?

Mrs O'Brien told me.

At the bus stop we meet another Polish lady and her son. Her name is Mrs Tekla Milcz and her son's name is Andrzej. Call him Andrew, she says to me. They, too, are returning to the railway station. Andrew and I nod to each other respectfully but he seems shy and it takes him a while to begin talking freely. I notice he turns away from us a lot and stares in the opposite direction. By the time the bus arrives, however, we have learnt that they arrived in Australia a year before us and live in Granville. Her husband, Oleg, was a lawyer in Lithuania, but now works for Murray Brothers in Parramatta. Mrs Milcz is a very beautiful woman and seems like she has come from an aristocratic family. When we get off to change trains at Lidcombe, Andrew and I have talked and found we both like drawing and painting, and collecting pictures of wrestlers from the newspapers. We say that we'll be friends when school goes back and bring in our wrestling scrapbooks to show each other.

My mother and I don't talk very much after that. The weather's still hot and I feel sleepy. It's a ten-minute wait for our train. I keep thinking about the fight, about Charley and Anthony, about Andrew and his mother. I ask my mother, Do you think I'll be friends with those boys when I grow old and turn thirty or forty? My mother replies, I'm sure you will ... Anyway, it's all in God's hands.

The carriage is half-empty and the train continues to rattle and jolt even after it picks up speed. My mother is quiet; her eyes are closed. I ask, What are you thinking about, Mum?

Roses, she says. I had a dream once that I died and went to Heaven. It was all roses!

Roses

My mother grew roses
whose names
belonged to a different era —
Apollo, Montezuma, Mr Lincoln,
whose petals and whorls
gave off such reflections
you'd shield your eyes
in mid-summer
as you walked through
the front garden.

They grew like aristocrats
in rows and circular plots
behind bricks
and grey paling fences —
those magnificent presences
that somehow gave
our suburban lives
a different kind of meaning.

People returning home
from the factories
in the afternoon
would stop to smell them
or comment on their beauty.
"Have some," my mother
would offer. "I have plenty."
She cared for her roses
with the same attention
you might in rearing a child —
watering, feeding, pruning,
knowing what needed doing
and what time of the year
it had to be done.

My mother never studied
history or mythology,
never debated what
immortality might mean.
Her home was her castle
and she was content
to work among roses to the end —
remaining, in her own realm,
a woman who was neither
servant nor queen.

Last Performance

For the last Physical Culture performance at St Peter Chanel's, a group of ten boys was trained by Sister Anne to build a human pyramid by getting down on their hands and knees, first four, then three on top of four, then two on three, and finally one on top of two. As one of the heavier boys, I was on the second-bottom row with Ziggy and Freddy McAlpine. Our "top boy" was Stefan, small and light. He enjoyed clambering up on to the backs of the larger boys while they steadied themselves. Look at me, look at me, he would laugh, I'm a monkey!

You're a nut! Donny yelled back from the bottom row.

A coco-nut, Leon called out, also on the bottom row. Because of their size and weight, they were down there with Joseph Risotto and Gregory Hogan.

Boys, boys! poor Sister Anne, all flustered, would call, and come running.

Whenever we tumbled it was on to green grass. Bones hit bones, elbows connected with skulls, shoulders and arms hit the ground. There were no mats, nothing to cushion our falls. Apart from this display, Sister Anne also trained us in marching, captain ball, tunnel ball, relays, and novelty events such as three-legged races, egg-and-spoon races and bowling hoops. This pyramid was her crowning event, proof that she was a capable teacher, that she could train the boys of St Peter Chanel's to perform something special.

Sister clapped her hands and we sprang into action just as we'd done so many times at practice. This was the finale to the Physical Culture demonstration. It had to be perfect.

First row, second row, third row. All was going well. Now Stefan had to climb over our backs and shoulders, as our bones creaked and muscles hurt with the weight on them and the strain of concentrating and holding the formation together. The effort was as much mental as it was physical.

Stefan reached the top and stood there, arms held out, feet spread, in a star shape. For whatever reason, the pyramid began to shake more than it had at practice. Not just wobble, but shake.

Somebody on the bottom row was laughing, trying to hold it in, but laughing, shaking. We could feel the vibrations spreading up the pyramid.

There's an ant going up my nose, Donny called out. An ant's biting me. I've got to scratch my nose!

It was Leon who was shaking, trying hard not to laugh. Hope it goes right into your brain, he said to Donny.

How can it? asked Gregory. He doesn't have a brain.

Shut your faces, Donny yelled back. All of youse!

Hey, Stefan screamed, I'm going to fall.

Now we're all laughing, Ha ha ha!

Sister Brendan was glaring at us, going red in the face. Sister Anne looked embarrassed, sad. I thought she was going to cry. Father Donovan looked amused. The spectators couldn't believe their eyes. Some were smiling, some giggling, some looked scared.

Stefan came tumbling down first, crying as he hit the ground, My arm's broken! Ouch!

The two rows below him collapsed.

There were arms and legs and shoulders and heads everywhere, coming down on top of bodies, straight down and sideways, tangled up in each other. Sounds of laughter and pain came from every part of the jumble. Someone was crying. Someone laughing. There were grunts, groans, swearing.

Ouch, ouch!

Aah, oh, ah!

Hey, that's my head!

You don't have a head.

Who said that?

Not me.

Just wait, I'll find out.

Get off, I'm not a pincushion.

You look like one!

Ha ha!

I think my nose's broken.

That'll improve your looks.

What looks?

You oughta talk.

We straightened up, rearranged our clothes, a sorry lot of young athletes, wondering what lay in store for us. We knew we'd let down Sister Anne, and in our hearts we were sorry for her. This was supposed to be our moment of glory; instead it was going to end up as our day of shame. I hated to think what fate lay in store for us next day at school.

Donny whispered, Gee, I'm sorry, fellas.

Wait'll I get my hands on you, Leon hissed. I'm going to rub my bruises into your face.

The playground suddenly became a sea of applause, an eruption of clapping, cheering and whistling that hit us like a wave breaking on the beach, lifting us with its strength and holding us up high, shining in the sun, then dumping us back on to the sand, back to a different kind of reality.

The entire assembly, school children and visitors, was applauding us, even the nuns and Father Donovan.

We were stunned. Left speechless.

Donny whispered just loud enough for the pyramid boys to hear, There wasn't any ant. Fooled youse!

Stefan yelled out, What did you say? He broke formation, ran straight at Donny and gave him a dead leg. You nearly busted my arm! he was screaming. Take that!

Hey, watch it, squirt! Donny rubbed his thigh, trying to pretend that it didn't hurt. He pushed Stefan away.

Don't shove me around, you liar, Stefan answered back, throwing a punch and hitting Donny on the arm.

That's it. You asked for it, you little pipsqueak.

Before you could blink twice they were both rolling on the ground, swearing at each other, throwing punches, missing more than they were connecting.

Donny was bigger and stronger than Stefan, and so Leon and Ziggy and I ran over to help him. Blindly, we threw ourselves into the brawl. As we did, I felt a fist hit me in the mouth and I tasted blood, hot, as it ran from my bottom lip. Hell's bells, I cried, I was only trying to help Stefan!

Once again there were arms and legs in a tangle. Punches were collecting me in the head, on my back and on my neck. This was serious. All ten boys had now joined in the fighting. We were all trying to help one another. Leon was laughing his head off. This was fun. Hey, Greg, stop picking your nose! Can you believe it, he's picking his nose instead of fighting?

A whistle was blown over our heads, loud and long, and into our ears.

Sister Brendan, of course! Who else?

All of you, break it up, you bold, brazen lads! Such disgraceful behaviour in front of your parents and visitors and Father Donovan himself. Such un-Christian-like behaviour! What would the Lord and the Mother of God think if they were here?

They'd think Donny was a rat, Sister, for doing what he did, said Stefan, wiping his face. They'd think Gregory was rude for picking his nose in public, too. He did, Sister, honestly he did. It was during the fight but we all saw him, didn't we, didn't we?

We all nodded while Gregory took deep breaths, his eyes two black smouldering coals beneath his thick black eyebrows. Shut your face or I'll shut it. Little wog!

Gregory, mind your language! Sister said. Or you'll have your mouth washed out with soap.

Father Donovan strode over like Old King Cole, big and important, waving his arms, restoring calm. The school spectators were cheering and whistling again, obviously having enjoyed the fight. Some men were calling out, More, more! Let 'em slug it out!

Now, boys, said Father, we'll be having no more of that. Let's see you all shake hands with the boy next to you ... Like he's just brought you a bag of lollies and he's your best friend ... Come, now, Gregory, Terence, Joseph ... That's it, all of you, shake hands.

We all shook hands, some seriously, others trying not to laugh.

Thank you, boys ... Oh thank you all, each and every one. Sister Anne was running over to us. I'm so proud of you all. She'd been forgotten in the fight and there she stood now, like an angel, wringing her hands, weeping with gratitude.

Off we went in all directions, like lambs or calves that've been separated from their mothers, returning instinctively to where we knew our parents waited, in whichever part of the paddock, some of us with bloodied noses, with bruises, with scratches, skinned knees and elbows. Never mind, our parents would say, you are all heroes, the pyramid boys who made the impossible possible.

There they go, Sister, Father Donovan was saying as he waved us off, the future leaders of Australia.

Would you be coming to the convent for a wee dram of refreshment, Father?

Why, thank you, Sister, yes, I will avail myself of your kind invitation ... Yes, and why not? A little drop in the tumbler would be just the thing at the end of an unforgettable day in the life of our parish. First I must say farewell to some of the parishioners, if I may?

Certainly, Father, whenever you are ready ... My, my, won't it be a grand day when this bunch of little hooligans marches off to high school?

Now, now, Sister, boys will be boys ...

II

Bullseye!

Something in the vegetable garden behind the garage catches my eye. The small gate is dilapidated, hanging to its post by one hinge, but it still manages to stay attached to the picket fence.

It's a "lucky stone" — one of those flat, polished stones you find in riverbeds or in watercourses. How did it get here? It's probably been in the soil for years and has now come to the surface. Picking it up, I turn it over, as if I expect to find something rare.

The colour is a pale grey, with a swirl of white around its edge in a marbling effect. Lying flat in my right palm, it resembles a miniature flying saucer, waiting for a command.

Without a second thought as to why I'm doing it, I pick it up in my left hand and send it spinning over the back fence, hoping, as I bite my bottom lip and hold my breath, that it will land in Duck Creek. From the sound of grasses or weeds, I know it does.

At first it spun and swerved horizontally, inscribing an upward arc, before levelling out. Still spinning, it fell forward quickly, until I lost sight of it over the fence. That was when I listened for the sound of it hitting the ground. That was when I heard myself cry out "Bullseye!", forty-four or forty-five years earlier.

Before Mary Street was settled fully there was an abundance of bushland on both sides. We lived on the western side, and in front of our house there were two vacant blocks, heavily over-grown with gum trees. A track — a shortcut to the shops and railway station — connected Mary Street to Elaine Street be-hind these blocks.

Three of us were playing on the vacant blocks with shang-hais, trying to hit birds and cats or dogs that happened to come into view. There was a boldness in that kind of venture that adults would condemn as careless. Nice boys didn't shoot at birds and try to hit other people's pets. In those days, there was nothing nice about us because we were *wogs*, foreigners, and children of *Bloody Balts* from across the sea who were dis-placing the *True-Blue Aussies*. It didn't matter when the True-Blue Aussies' sons and daughters committed violations against Nature or Society. However, because we spoke a dif-ferent language and ate black bread and salted herrings, we were different and our actions were often frowned upon and derided. So we learnt to retaliate with defiance, bravado, wilful acts of disobedience. As we grew into adulthood we would learn that this was the wrong way to go about proving our-selves. We were to discover that success at school and in the workforce counted for a lot more than retaliation with stones and sticks.

The O'Sullivans lived in Elaine Street and had two daugh-ters, Christine and Lynette. Mrs O'Sullivan was small as a mouse; she walked with her head tilted to one side, as if her neck was paralysed. When I passed her in the street she would swivel her body around, look up, say, Oh, it's you. Hello, then she'd break into a giggling fit. I truly believed that she was slow-witted. Once I laughed a reply behind her back, Ha-ha, and ran off. She waved a finger at me and threatened, I'll tell your mother, you know, I will. She giggled, screwing up her thin face as she did, balanced herself on her toes, pirouetted a full circle and continued walking away from me.

Mr O'Sullivan was an accountant who worked in the city. Dressed in a white shirt and black tie, he wore arm bands and his sleeves rolled down. Fully dressed in a black suit he looked like an undertaker. He carried a wooden brief case to and from work. Short like his wife, he walked with a briskness that made it seem like he'd been wound up. His hair was combed back, slick and impeccably clean, like Mandrake the Magician's.

Some altercation occurred between Christine O'Sullivan and me. She was pointing from her front gate at me, taunting, laughing, Go on, I dare you! Bet you can't hit me, bet you can't!

Go on, said Stefan and Ziggy together. Go on …

I didn't bother putting the lucky stone I'd picked up into my shanghai; it flew from my hand like it had received a papal blessing. Nothing was going to stop it.

Bullseye! Ziggy and Stephan yelled together, slapping their thighs and gasping, as Christine O'Sullivan put her hand to her forehead and dropped to her knees as if she'd been poleaxed. Her sister screamed and ran into their house. I was in big trouble.

It just couldn't happen!

How?

How could I have hit Christine O'Sullivan from such a distance? And, as I was to find out afterwards, right between the eyes.

I took off as fast as my legs would carry me, first into the house and then into the bush, my shanghai inside my shirt, out of sight. Bullseye or no bullseye, there was no way in the world I was going to surrender it. Stefan and Ziggy came with me, providing logic and solace with phrases like, She'll be okay, don't worry. Or, Mate, at least you didn't kill her. The truth was — and I knew it — that I was in plenty of hot water. Silly small Mrs O'Sullivan didn't worry me, but once my mother discovered what I'd done, that was it!

When Stefan and Ziggy left and quiet returned to the bush, I came out of my hiding place and returned home. The dog met me on the back steps and licked my hands and face in sympathy. In my mind's eyes, all I could see was Christine hitting the ground on her knees, hands up to her face. Hell, what if I'd scarred her for life? Somehow damaged her permanently? What if her parents took me to court? What if … What if …

My father returned from work first and changed into his home work clothes. I managed to avoid him, or at least to avoid his eyes.

Nothing's wrong? he asked.

No, I lied. Why do you ask?

You seem strange. Are you sick or something?

Sick! My stomach was turning like a cement mixer! How could he tell? No, I'm not, I lied again.

Alright. Stay inside if you want to — but put the dog outside.

Bobby went outside promptly, wagging his tail, down to his kennel. I read comics in my bedroom until I heard my mother returning. She would change her clothes as well, then busy herself with the preparation of dinner. In the summer months, when light lasted longer, first of all she would help my father in the garden. While he dug rows of earth she would plant seeds or seedlings. Sometimes they argued over what should go where, but no matter how drastically their opinions differed, they would end up agreeing. Afterwards, the whole garden would be watered.

No sooner did I hear her moving about in the kitchen than there was a loud knocking on the back door.

I could hear Mrs O'Sullivan's voice calling, Mrs … Mrs … !

She couldn't pronounce our surname and mangled it as she continued knocking at the door. Mrs … !

My mother went running through the house like it was on fire. I could hear Mrs O'Sullivan's raised voice, see her contorted face in my mind's eye as she blurted out the accusation. I heard my name called out sternly in Polish.

Mrs O'Sullivan and Christine stood at the back door; Bobby was licking Christine's hand and she was smiling through her tears, patting the dog's head. Between her eyes was a purple lump the shape and size of a thimble. I had expected it to be bigger.

Sparrows were twittering among the tomato rows, playing their own games.

He nearly killed my daughter, Mrs ... Her pronunciation sounded like *Skaznatski* or *Skanerski* ... Look, will you — oh, just look, will you!

My father walked over and stood with a hoe in his hand, his hat pushed back on his head.

Bobby was sniffing around Mrs O'Sullivan's ankles.

Did you do this? my mother snapped at me, pointing at Christine's forehead.

Yes, I said, but she dared me to.

Wait here. She whipped around and walked into the kitchen directly behind us.

I heard one of the drawers being opened. Cutlery rattled.

She came out with one hand behind her back.

Apologise to Christine!

No! She dared me.

Apologise! Her voice was raised. Her mouth was set. She was breathing quickly.

No!

Apologise, Peter. My father spoke gently but firmly, nodding his head; it was his way of coaxing words out of me.

My mother was having none of this playing around. For the last time, apologise.

For the last time, I blurted out, no!

Her hand appeared in less than an eye-blink takes and the wooden spoon connected with the back of my right leg. I will remember that flat sound of wood on skin for the rest of my life. My leg stung immediately; it felt hot and it was burning.

The faces before me were watery, blurry, and I knew I was trying to see them through my tears. Mrs O'Sullivan stepped back, grabbed Christine's hand and started to leave.

No! my mother cried. He has not yet apologised. Turning to me, she commanded, Apologise!

No! Never. Not as long as I live!

In swift succession two more smacks followed on the other leg and I was apologising to Christine, her mother, the dog, my father and the rest of the world — anybody and anything that cared to listen. I didn't care anymore.

Now, my mother said calmly, the punishment is over. He has apologised and will go to his room. You two may go home. I am very sorry about what he did. Christine's swelling will go down and one day they will be friends again. Luckily, the skin was not broken.

All of a sudden Mrs O'Sullivan was jumping up and down, screaming, shooing Bobby away. Oh, goodness me! Look at what the filthy dog's done. He's wet my shoe ... You people, what sort of country did you come from? Your animals are just like you — barbaric! ... Come on, darling, let's get out of here. She grabbed Christine's hand and stormed out of the garden, up the side of the house, slamming the gate behind her. Just as they disappeared from view, Christine turned around and poked her tongue out at me.

My father came over and put his arm around my shoulders. Come on, he said. Take Bobby with you and go to your room or help me out the back — whichever you prefer. My mother disappeared into the house. I wanted to hate her, to yell at her and blame her for the minutes of pain and shame. If I stayed outside with Dad I knew she would follow shortly, so I went to my room and curled up with Bobby, rubbing the backs of my legs. They were red. They hurt. They had welts. Bobby licked them and gradually the pain ebbed away. Or maybe it just felt like the pain wasn't there ... At least Bobby was on my side.

Hey, Bobby, that was pretty good — peeing on the old witch's shoe. Thanks. I was laughing, unable to stop myself. Bobby wagged his tail madly.

That evening I was called to dinner formally. My mother

knocked on my bedroom door and told me that food was ready. We ate in the kitchen, at a small round table that folded in the middle so that it became semi-circular. The flat side was placed against the wall and we ate in those three places for as long as we lived in 10 Mary Street: my father in the far corner between the walls; my mother in the middle so that access to the stove and sink was easiest for her; me, because I am left-handed, directly opposite my father, next to the door that opened into the dining–lounge room area.

The welts on my legs had turned from dark red to a kind of light orange colour, tinged with purple. But the marks still hurt and I wasn't going to pretend that they didn't. All my life, even now, unless I am at somebody's home or out in public, when I sit down I automatically put my right leg under me and sit on it. Comfortable as a cushion. This time I couldn't because it meant sitting on the welts.

We talked about the day, about my father travelling to and from work, about my mother cleaning the homes of the O'Brien and the O'Neil families. She remarked on the number of bedrooms in many of these big houses in Strathfield she had cleaned, how heavy the vacuum cleaners were to carry upstairs and how the numerous children sometimes drove her to annoyance. She had favourites in these two households, two small boys, Paul and Michael, who confided all the family secrets to her and loved her like an aunty. She loved them in return, and would take extra doughnuts and potato dumplings from our kitchen for them to share with her while she had her lunch.

None of us mentioned the incident with Christine.

I wasn't game enough to bring up the subject and my parents carried on as if nothing unusual had happened that afternoon. When we finished eating I was told to go and have my bath and get ready for bed. That part of the evening was normal. After my bath I usually did my homework, read comics or a book or listened to radio serials.

Both parents came to see me together when I was in bed. Usually they came in separately to say goodnight.

About this evening, my father said. It should not have happened ...

She dared me! I interjected, almost yelling it out, and for a moment it seemed that the scene with the wooden spoon was to be repeated.

It should not have happened as it did ... He picked up the sentences calmly, wisely, as if he knew beforehand that I was going to interrupt.

Throwing the stone at Christine was wrong — and yes, we know that she dared you — but defying your mother and father was a different kind of wrong.

How?

It's called disobedience, my mother said. You don't say *no* to your parents, especially in front of someone who could cause us trouble. You know what a lot of Australians think about migrants. You have seen plenty of evidence of it. Why don't you remember that next time and create a good example?

In the Ten Commandments you are told to *Honour* "your father and your mother", are you not? my father asked.

Yes, I replied meekly. Somehow mentioning the Ten Commandments meant God and all the divine power that God could use against you. Hell?... Fire?... Eternal punishment?... Pain?... My mouth barely opened and the words crept out like a cautious mouse. I'm sorry, Mum and Dad. Sorry that I disobeyed you. As soon as the apology was spoken my mother put her arms around me, gave me a hug and comforted me, and so did my father. The pain from the welts was non-existent. The incident of the afternoon dissolved in another watery blur.

Coming out into the garden next day felt strange, leaving by the front gate and walking through the vacant allotment from where I'd thrown the stone. There were bruises on the backs of my legs.

Judy is in the lounge room. The TV is turned off and she's taken out Mum's photo albums.

One album has a white cover, another is blue, a third is red and the fourth, the slimmest, has an image of the Sydney Botanic Gardens on front and back covers. In the background rises the Opera House and the top of the Harbour Bridge. It's the kind of album made for tourists. When did my mother buy it? Perhaps she was attracted to the bright flowers on the covers, the palm trees, green grass and flowerbeds of salvias, marigolds and petunias — the kinds of flowers that she grew in her own front garden.

Judy is holding up a black-and-white photograph. Look at this one, Dad — you were so little.

Between closing of the garage and returning to the house, I have calculated that it is seventy-eight days since my mother died.

Seven plus eight equals fifteen. One plus five equals six. Six is the number of the house I live in. Six is the day wrongly given as my birth date by Frau Horst, the German midwife who registered my birth. It was in the last days of the Third Reich. Money was running out. To qualify for her payment the midwife added me to the list of babies born the previous week. She received her money and I became a day older. My mother recounted that story, without regret, many times. I would complain that this shouldn't have been done. My mother asked me to try and see it from the woman's point of view. She explained that an extra day didn't really matter to one's life. I disagreed and still do. When I travelled to Germany in 1989, into that district in the north known as Westphalia, and, more specifically, as *Das Sauerland*, and met the midwife, she gave me the gift that my mother had sent her some time after she was moved into one of the Displaced Persons' camps in Germany: a photograph of my mother and myself.

The one that Judy is holding.

I am between eighteen months and two years old. There are thistles or prickly weeds of some kind growing out of sandy soil, almost surrounding us. It would appear that I am sitting in these, but in fact I am leaning against my mother who has put her head against mine. She is smiling; I am frowning. A small posey has been pinned above my left pocket. She has dressed me in lace-up booties, long white socks; my shorts are buttoned to my shirt and two of the large buttons shine like polished coins. My hair is neatly combed. She is wearing what she would have called "a good dress". A large thick clump of weeds is growing in the foreground like a sea anemone. She is holding my right hand in her right hand, probably telling me to smile. As with the Christmas photograph, I wonder who took this one? Why did my mother choose it to send to the midwife? When the old woman returned it to me in 1989, she said, in broken English, *Now you can tell your mother, because I have seen you, she can have it back.* She saw me looking at the letter in her hand, a letter from the same envelope out of which she'd taken the photograph. *But not the letter. I will keep the letter.* When I examined the letter I knew immediately it was in my mother's handwriting. Forty years hadn't changed it that much, plus there was her name signed at the bottom. Another surprise was seeing the letter written in German. Until recently, when my mother re-established contact with the people who were her employers in Germany during World War II, I never knew that she could write in German, although I had heard her speak the language as I was growing up. Later, in Australia, when I questioned her about the letter, she replied nonchalantly that it was something she'd learnt in Germany before and during the war, but now she had forgotten it mostly. Returning the photograph and showing me the letter seemed to have been important for Frau Horst — as if she were keeping her part of a pact made between them.

While we were talking her son came in. He'd been living in

Bavaria and had returned to his mother's house for the summer. He explained this, or at least I believed that was what he was saying, as well as telling me he was a hunter and one day would come to Australia to do some hunting. He was a giant of a man, huge, barely fitting through the doors of the house. He had to stoop in order to pass from room to room. When we shook hands, my hand must have fitted into a quarter of his palm. Sensing my discomfort, he let go quickly and his booming laughter filled the house.

At one point in the meeting, both mother and son saw me looking at an aerial photograph on the wall. Dark green predominantly, it is of a mountain valley. Grey roads snake through it and divide blocks of cleared land on which homes have been built. Red and white shapes. Roofs. Houses. In the middle, slightly in the upper left corner, is "The White House" — the house in which my mother worked. I have already been shown her room, a gabled outlook upon trees and hills, its roof so low, and at an angle, that one has to stoop. I will learn that German law was changed at one point during the war and servants who were not Germans were not allowed to live in the same house as their masters. That is when my mother was moved out and into her permanent quarters. Across the road from the house, through the trees, runs a small track, quite discernible, and it leads downhill to a factory. Behind the factory is a row of green huts, "barracks", as my mother referred to them. At the end of this row, in the last two rooms, are my mother's quarters. Members of the family who employed my mother have been acting as my hosts. They have shown me over the house and the barracks, and brought me to the midwife.

Frau Horst sees me continuing to look at the photograph. Would you like to have it? she asks.

I can't answer because there's a lump in my throat.

Have it — take it! her son calls out. Leaps up. He takes me by the hand again, as if to congratulate me, and his booming laughter fills the room like a depth-charge echo. I can get another one! He takes the picture down from the wall, out of its frame and puts it with my bag. Your first home in the world — all ready to go to Australia!

The photograph is associated with the deepest memory I have, not just of Germany, but of life itself, the memory that has troubled me and of which I couldn't speak for decades, until a meeting in 1969 with Doctor Frank Croll, a doctor who was treating me for burst ulcers in Sydney, brought my first remembered utterance about it.

Today the aerial photograph hangs in my office, to the left of the desk where I work, above photographs of my family and various friends.

What's the matter, Dad? Judy asks. You seem upset. What's wrong?

Nothing. I'm not upset about anything.

I explain how the photograph came into our possession and why it's so special, but then, I think, aren't all of these photographs special? There must be images in those four albums that I haven't seen for years, maybe decades. We sit on the couch and begin looking through them.

There is no special order or arrangement, although in one my mother has written in Polish, in the index, three entries, all dated 9.11.86. Translated, the names of the photographs read, sequentially, *front of house, Feliks and Peter in front of kitchen, side of the house from the street.*

Then it strikes me. The date! It's her birthday! The ninth of November! She began these entries on her birthday in 1986! Was the album a birthday gift from someone — or something she'd saved up for a special occasion?

We turn the pages and confront scenes from both our lives that are strange and familiar. My father nursing Judy on the front lawn under the rose bushes. Both are smiling. Her chubby cheeks are apple-red and her dress is pink. She is holding something black, possibly a purse or a cuddly toy. My father is wearing his brown Akubra hat and has his sleeves rolled up. The date on the back reads 20.10.1973. That means Judy is seventeen months old. Alongside that photograph is a smaller one, taken on a Kodak Instamatic camera, one of my father holding my son, Andrew. The inscription and date on the back reads *Mother's Day 11.5.75.* Andrew is thirteen months old, plump as a potato, and is lying back, securely cradled in my father's left arm, pleased as Punch, smiling almost demurely. What does that smile mean?

My father is wearing a grey-blue cardigan and a blood-red corduroy shirt. The shirt matches the red sleeves of Andrew's pullover and the red, white and blue checks of the pattern on his chest. The photograph was taken in the back yard of 10 Mary Street, in between two adjacent walls. The green and white patterns of the pillow on the reclining deck chair contrast with the red bricks in the background. Behind all this, a white downpipe, appearing out of nowhere and disappearing the same way, runs the length of the brick wall like a broadsword.

So it goes, delving further into the past, with leaps into forgotten scenes and an array of faces from the Ukraine, Poland, the Displaced Persons' camps in Germany and the migrant camps in Australia — photographs taken in Regents Park, Bankstown, Strathfield, Lidcombe, Bondi, Shellharbour, places where we have lived, worked, visited or played. Parents. Children. My wife. My ex-wife. Relatives. Friends. Faces whose names I have forgotten. Faces whose names I will never forget. Young. Old. Christenings. Birthdays. First Holy Communion. Weddings. Funerals. Indoor settings and outdoor settings. Group photographs and people posing alone or in pairs.

A small rectangular photograph shows me sitting, barefooted, legs stretched out, in a garden alongside another small boy, also barefooted. A ladder has been propped against a wall behind us; a retaining wall runs below a dense row of foliage. The grass is thick and we are sitting on a blanket. The other boy is holding a section of a newspaper in one hand, as if offering it. His blond hair falls over his forehead and he is biting his bottom lip, squinting. He is wearing shorts and a cardigan that is unbuttoned. My shirt is long-sleeved, buttoned to the neck. My black hair contrasts with his and I am wearing a pair of knitted trousers with bib and braces. Another part of the newspaper is folded over my legs. The date on the back of the photograph reads 30 September 1950.

I am five years old. The blond-haired boy's name is Allan, and he is the same boy that I argued with and then cried because I felt left out when he received a toy carpentry set for his birthday.

The next photograph that Judy points out is of Anna, her half-sister (my mother has written *Anna 2 years* underneath it). Anna is standing behind her stroller with her doll, Cindy, in it. There is a brown-and-white cuddly toy on Cindy's lap. Cindy's plastic shoes are red, her socks are white and her dress is pink and white. Anna is wearing red socks, white sandals, pink tracksuit pants, a red skivvy and a floral pinafore made up of hibiscus patterns. They are in the back garden of 10 Mary Street and in front of one of the camellia bushes growing outside the kitchen window. When I come over to water the garden after my mother's death, it is the camellia bushes that get watered first. Clusters of petals have fallen to the ground, creating a carpet over the sandstone and soil of the garden bed. Behind the camellia bush, almost obscured, is a tall fuschia bush, its red and purple flowers drooping like bells.

Like Judy in her photograph, Anna has chubby cheeks. Her face, round as a ripe peach, is almost serious, halfway between enquiring and bemused. She knows she is the centre of attention here, in charge of the scene, and she will maintain that pose no matter what else might happen. As they grow older, I have begun to notice how similar Andrew and Anna are in their attitudes and habits, in their control of a moment. Both can be supreme, intractable. The earth could shudder, trees fall, a tidal wave appear on the horizon, yet neither would flinch, retreat from their stand, change their facial expression.

What are you thinking, Dad?

Falling trees and tidal waves.

Huh?

Never mind.

Dad, do you want to have some lunch?

Sure, why not? I'm glad the topic is changed. I suggest to her we drive up to Kentucky Fried at Yagoona and bring back some lunch. She agrees.

At Yagoona, however, we decide to eat there, to sit at one of the front tables and watch the traffic on the Hume Highway. The flow of motor vehicles is nonstop, even on this, a public holiday, even with traffic lights at the top of the hill to our right, and to our left, slightly further towards the railway station.

I tell her about an old school friend, Malcolm MacGregor, who lived at Yagoona and whose home I used to visit on weekends.

He had a dental plate in his top front teeth and would slip it in and out of his mouth whenever he wanted to shock someone at school or make us laugh … and laugh we did. It was a novelty that never wore off. Funny how you remember things about people, and how people are associated with a place. If we hadn't decided to come to Yagoona, who knows how long it would have been before I thought of Malcolm McGregor again?

Have you got any photos of him?

I do — in the old *Lumens*, the school year-books of St Pat's.

Other memories are jogged by being here at this location, by the Hume Highway and the sight of shops opposite us. It was from here that I would purchase takeaway lunches for my mother whenever she expressed a wish to have chicken pieces for lunch. She believed in the taste of the "Colonel's" recipe of "secret" herbs and spices.

I think about this.

Secret? What does that mean? I don't believe secrets really exist. They are facts in the world that are only relative to what we know or don't know about life. Death annihilates life and life begets more life. I believe that is the great mystery, the "secret" of life. Once you have discovered that for yourself, there is no mystery.

We leave in silence, return to the empty house, shut up and grown warm in our absence.

I had hoped I might see some "diggers" on the streets, some hint of public activity to suggest the nature of this public holiday. Instead, I see plenty of Asian and Middle Eastern faces, ethnic types who have made Australia their home in the last three decades and settled permanently in this part of Sydney. I wonder what Anzac Day means to them? To their children? How are they celebrating it? How many of them attended the Dawn Service in Martin Place or marched down George Street?

Dad, I'm going to have to go, Judy says, almost apologetically.

Sure, that's fine … Whenever you're ready. I'll put away all these things. I've nothing else to do.

Are you sure you're alright?

Why wouldn't I be?

Oh, I don't know.

We say our goodbyes at the front door and I see her out into the street. I thank her for all her help, and for her company. I say, And *Babci* thanks you, too.

She drives off, slows down at the end of the street and waves. The car horn sounds its *beep beep* and she is gone, right into Clapham Road and off towards her home in Merrylands.

I return to the house and pack the photo albums into the linen press. But as I close the linen press door, a realisation strikes me. All the photographs that I scrutinised with Judy were of children, my children and myself as a child. Was this intentional? I don't remember consciously choosing the photos I deliberated over. Was I searching for some resemblance between them and myself?

The colours of the carpet beneath my feet acquire a life, begin to move, as if on a conveyor belt. Yet I am stationary.

I am sweating. My mother's presence fills the space to my left, the entrance to her bedroom. She is beside me, watching, but saying nothing. She is not the old woman who died in February. She is young, dressed in floral colours, a bright summer dress. Her hair is dark, thick, wavy. She is beautiful. She stands looking down, as if to examine what I'm doing. But *what* am I doing?

The colours begin to slow down and return to static patterns on a carpet. The giddiness has stopped. The sweating continues. My hands continue to perform whatever it is they were doing, as if they have become disembodied. Wiping my eyes, I see that I am undoing the brown bag, flicking through the photo albums until I find the photograph from Germany, the gift from Frau Horst. I put it into my shirt pocket. The bag is stowed in the linen cupboard and I shut it with an extra hard push.

All I can see in my mind is a little boy staring at me from an old black-and-white photograph. Turned inwards, in my shirt pocket, his image is facing my heart. His mother is trying to make him smile. She is wearing the same dress that my mother wore when she stood beside me at the linen cupboard. The little boy is frowning. He seems troubled. Is it the weather? The photographer? The clump of weeds he is sitting among?

Failings

The entry in my journal reads:

To Milperra. Faxed poems to RR and had interview with JK re her honours. A bit of shopping for Mum. And banking. Warm day. Andrew to work. In the evening Mum rang and said she'd had a bad attack of asthma. I went over and stayed about an hour and a half. She seemed okay after that. I wonder if it isn't some kind of mental fear or anxiety. The house is all closed up, stuffy, dark. I said, It's like a tomb. She said she feels cold otherwise. Returned home just after 9.30!!

After returning home from doing my mother's shopping and banking I'd decided to do some gardening. It was Daylight Saving Time and by mid-afternoon it had become one of those stinking hot February days. Sweat poured off me. Dirt was ingrained in the pores of my skin and under my fingernails. The lawnmower started after much frustration and swearing from me! Weeds were gathered and left to dry out on a mound. Grass cuttings were gathered and heaped in barrowloads and taken up to the very end of the yard where, together with the weeds, they'd decompose with mulching leaves. In due course, the compost would be spread out over the yard, recycled, returned to the earth it'd come from and out of which the grass and weeds would grow once more. It was a time when, because of the size of the yard, it would take me two days to do it all, end to end. Jija, our family dog, kept me company all afternoon, following me around from one task to another, running up and barking at birds that would land in the yard, then returning, tail wagging madly, flopping down next to me.

Around six o'clock my mother telephoned, asking me if I would come and stay the night; she'd had a bad asthma attack in the afternoon and believed she might need assistance during the night. Since my father's death, two-and-a-half years earlier, there'd been instances when I'd stay the night, or, at her request, stay into the late hours of the night and keep her company until she was ready to go to bed.

In a way, the call didn't surprise me and, to a degree, I felt annoyed about it coming at the time that it did. I was tired, needed a bath and wanted to relax after the gardening session in the hot afternoon sun. I wasn't particularly hungry but my main cause of complaint was having to get into the car and drive. Peak-hour traffic would've been over, but traffic is traffic. If I'm not in the mood for it, I loathe it.

My mother had made several such calls in recent months, some early in the morning, others at night, but I always responded. Towards the end of the previous year, for example, one morning she rang to say there'd been a break-in at her home during the night.

A break-in, Mum? How do you know?

Because your father's watch is missing.

Dad's watch?

It's not there.

Where?

By the bed. You know I use it when I have to check my ventilator times. It's not there. Come and call the police.

Call the police?

Do I have to get a neighbour to help me?

For goodness' sake, of course you don't. Just sit tight. I'll stop in on the way to work.

Hurry up. The robbers might still be around. I'm not going

out of the house until you get here. I've looked everywhere and it's not where I left it.

It might be in your bedclothes — or it's fallen off the bed.

I've looked everywhere.

It's there, Mum. Somewhere.

Are you calling me a liar?

No, Mum … Just wait. I'll be there shortly.

So I drove over, and found her distressed, shaken and worried.

Let's search for it together, I said.

I've searched already. Just call the police.

Okay. I'll call the police after one more search.

To this, she agreed. I turned the bedclothes over several times. No watch. Not on the floor? I asked.

I've looked but the bed's so low and I can't get under.

Getting right down on my hands and elbows — backside up in the air — I immediately saw the object of her consternation. But how the devil did she get it so far under the bed?

It's there, Mum. I reached as far as I could and was just able to get my fingers to the band.

Here's your watch, Mum, I said, handing it to her while still on the floor. See, all safe and sound. There weren't any robbers. You must have dropped it when you checked the time, then you could have accidentally kicked it under the bed when you got out … Everything's okay.

I stood up, straightened myself and turned around happily. Instead of a smile on the face of my mother, I saw sadness on the face of an old woman, shoulders slouched, head bowed, tears rolling down her cheeks. The end of her shawl hung down and forward, like a mask, partly obscuring her face. She looked like a child admitting to a mistake and awaiting punishment.

I'm just a silly old woman, she sobbed. I'm so ashamed. Please forgive me.

Mum, Mum, there's nothing to forgive. You did nothing

wrong. I hugged her, gave her a kiss and held her, hearing the ticking of her alarm clock that seemed to sound extra loud. Gradually she brightened up. She wiped her face with a crumpled hankie that she took from her dressing gown pocket and looked at the watch in her hand.

Your father would be having a good laugh right now, you know.

You think so?

He loved this watch. It's a Seiko. A good watch. It will be yours someday.

I know. And the Unicorn one that you gave me back in 1968, it's still good. I'll wear them both.

At the same time?

Always. One on each hand.

We both laughed — she wiping away her tears, me with the awareness of a strange knowledge that I'd just participated in the enactment of a tableau, a prelude to something more traumatic than I'd ever experienced in my life.

On the drive to work this feeling persisted, wouldn't leave. My mother was safe, in her home, probably saying the rosary that I saw in her hands when we said goodbye at the front door — but I also knew that something was passing away between us and our lives would never be the same. She needed me as never before but wouldn't come out and say it. I, the grown son, had to accept the fact that in her eyes I was still the little boy in the photograph taken in a Displaced Persons' camp in Germany, the little boy sitting in a patch of weeds, being cuddled by a beautiful dark-haired young woman, proudly holding her frowning son's hand.

Flicking back through the pages of my 1997 journal I found the two entries that I was searching for. I read and reread them.

Monday, 6 January 1997

To Milperra. E-mails and computing. Shopping for Mum and lunch. Mum rang late in evening to say the wind's blown in her garage door. I went over. She was very stressed. Also depressed. And lonely. I think she's getting worse. Is obsessive about tidiness and having all the little things done around the house. I secured the door and got home about 10.30 p.m. Very distressed about my mother. I feel she wants me there all the time. She feels insecure when she's on her own too long.

Tuesday, 7 January 1997

Mum ran again this morning. Her ventilator was dancing around (up and down) so that it fell to the floor. She reckons there's a ghost in the house. She feels that a spirit has entered the house. Talked a while. Said I'll be over tomorrow.

As we talked about my coming over on that evening in February because of her asthma, I vividly remembered the three incidents: the misplaced watch, the garage door that'd been blown off its hinges by a strong wind and the ventilator "dancing around" before her eyes. Had my mother been hallucinating? Had her medication affected her adversely, making her imagine persecutions and break-ins? Maybe if I talked to her she would calm down. Again she asked if I would come over, stay the night and go early in the morning.

Because of daylight saving, it was still light at six o'clock, and I hadn't cleaned myself from the gardening or had any dinner. Okay, Mum, I said. Give me a little time and I'll be over.

I had a bath, ate a small meal, packed my pyjamas, toiletries, reading glasses and a book. I told my family I'd be back as soon as possible. In the morning I had to travel to Alexandria, to Hale & Iremonger, to collect the last of the remaindered copies of my novel *The Beloved Mountain*. Because of traffic flows, I planned to set out after peak hour and return during the noonday hours when there seems to be a drop in the volume of traffic on the roads.

Mum was in good spirits when I arrived and had been watching the ABC *News*. She said she hadn't eaten but wasn't hungry. The idea of eating food nauseated her, she said, and dismissed the idea with a wave of her hand. Watch *This Day Tonight* with me, will you? she asked. We sat on the lounge at either end like we did in the days when I lived there. She turned off the main lights because it was wasting electricity, she claimed, and we sat in semi-darkness, the room illuminated by the TV screen's glow and the light from her milk-glass lamp on the sideboard in one corner of the room.

The talk turned to the past, especially to memories of what her life had been like since Dad died.

At first I thought it would be easy, she said. The pressure gone, you know, of looking after him. His tantrums were getting worse. He wasn't a young man. Feeding him, helping to wash him, dressing him, often not getting a word of thanks.

Mum, he was nearly ninety. Getting senile. Dementia was setting in. We spoke in Polish but I had to explain what I meant using English words because I didn't know their equivalents in Polish: old age, anger, silences, rages for no apparent reason, loss of interest in clothes and food, ceasing to ask questions about his family, his life and relatives back in Poland. Worst of all, loss of memory.

The TV screen flickered with the volume turned down.

She sat for a while, not saying anything, then began to speak almost absentmindedly, yet quite deliberately. More recently it's been very lonely, and that part of it is getting worse for me. All those imaginings, of spirits being in the house, losing things ... You think I don't know. It's fear of getting old, of living alone, seeing your face in the mirror and knowing there's no escape ... I left your father because he couldn't be trusted, you know ... He wasn't faithful ... It wasn't an easy life those first three years, but it would've been worse with him ... Then I met Feliks ... He was a kind man ... Treated me like a lady and was good to you ... So life went on, all those years, overcoming one crisis after another, moving on ... Look what happened last year to me with the shingles, eh? At my age. Shingles! There were times I wanted to kill myself because of the pain ... But I knew I could never do that ... Germany, the war, the camps, going hungry, not sleeping because of an empty stomach ... Bringing you up alone those early years! All my life, never ever anything like those damn shingles. Why would God want to punish an old woman with shingles? The pain was a fire!

I don't know if it was God, Mum. It just happened. The doctors say you carried the virus in your body, that's all, then it broke out. A leftover from chicken pox.

Bah, what do the doctors know? Chicken pox! I had that when I was a girl. Virus! Huh! It was God's doing. I know about these things.

Sure, it was bad for you, but it's over now. No more shingles. And, yes, you did look after Dad, and I'm helping to care for you as best as I can.

What can you do? she asked philosophically. You have your own life and your own problems ... Work, children to bring up still, house to pay off. You shouldn't be looking after an old woman like me.

There was a sense of impending gloom in the air. You could feel it. Shadows played eerily over the walls, over our faces, our hands, our clothes. Colours from the images on the television. Grey, white, yellow, shades of green, red, violet. Real and surreal. We were both alive — yet we could have both been drowning in a sea of waterweeds or floating in the sky under a raincloud.

I suggested she have a meal. I would fix it for her.

Why, don't you think I can get myself some food? I have a

little bit of chicken and potatoes I can heat up. There's also some coleslaw.

When she returned she'd eaten in the kitchen. Out of the blue, she asked, What will you do with the house when I'm gone?

What do you want me to do with it?

Whatever's best for you.

Why are you asking me that now?

Now's the right time.

Are you serious, Mum? But she was serious. I realised the answer to my question before I even finished asking it.

Now I had another sensation in the room, a sense of eerie displacement, a cold quietness — as if a stranger had entered the room and sat invisibly between us, pushing us apart, or a door had been left open at the back of the house and cold was coming into the house, separating us. It was like Death had entered the room. I was becoming uncertain, perhaps even afraid of what was to follow.

She moved to the lounge chair opposite me. We were now face to face, at eye level. She said, You've been a good son, though you didn't listen to me as much as you should have — and that's probably my fault for not being strict enough with you.

I was, as the Irish say, gobsmacked. Just like I'd been hit by an invisible fist. Mum, what're you saying?

She continued to speak as if I didn't exist, almost as if she were speaking to herself — as if she had to say all this, right then and there. You have a heart of gold and there's nothing you wouldn't do for anyone. I've seen plenty of evidence of your kindness. But you're immature, even though you are a man. Inside you're still a child. You need to grow up.

Maybe I'm okay, Mum. Maybe I like being who or what I am. What I'm still becoming. Then it occurred to me that I was about to start an argument with my mother and I didn't want that. Not tonight. Not ever again ... Yes, Mum, whatever you say. Can I make us a cup of tea?

Yes, that would be nice, she agreed. The TV had been turned off and she suggested we watch a movie together. It was like the previous few moments had disappeared under the doorstep, out of our lives, and into the late summer darkness.

When I returned from the kitchen with the tea she'd turned off the chandeliers and we were back into the earlier semi-gloom. It was about half-past eight and a black-and-white movie was starting. *Citizen Kane*, starring Orson Welles.

He's a good actor, my mother said. I've always liked his movies.

Liked his movies? How many had she seen? How's your tea, Mum?

Fine, just fine. She spoke very delicately, deliberately accentuating her vowels, like an actor on stage, making sure she could be heard.

The movie began with its opening dark scenes. The voice of the narrator matched the gloom. A chill ran through me and I wondered if this was the right kind of movie to be watching. Repeatedly in movie surveys of the twentieth century or in post–World War II movie lists *Citizen Kane* ranks number one. Various reasons are given, ranging from its being a psychological drama and capturing the essence of a detective story to its being a milestone in movie-making. An old man lies alone in a mansion called Xanadu that he has built, an extraordinarily rich man whose wealth is too great to calculate. He utters one word, "Rosebud", and dies. From his hand falls one of those small crystal balls, a snowdome. It shatters.

We could feel the silences in between our sipping tea and the stirring with our spoons. More than that, we could hear the echoes of the silences. Darkness had enveloped the house and the lives of the two people inside it. Mother and son. Unspoken words floated in the air between them, their breathing, the beating of their hearts. Their thoughts were almost audible — linked to all that existed around them by the darkness and the silence. House. Plants. Flowers. Trees. Grass. Starlight. Cricket song. Frog croak. The waters of Duck Creek running through the reserve behind 10 Mary Street, Regents Park, through the bulrushes and the weeds ... Towards the Parramatta River ... Away ... Into the night ...

Suddenly, like a knife, my mother's voice cleft the silence. No, go home. What will be, will be ...

Just like that, out of the blue — or in this case, black — I was being sent home. But why, you wanted me to stay?

No, I feel fine now, my asthma's much better. But before you go you can help me get my ventilator ready for when I have to use it during the night. Turn off the TV, will you, I've seen this movie before.

But I haven't — not fully. Whenever I've watched it something's happened and I've never found out who or what Rosebud was.

Doesn't matter. You'll have other chances to watch it.

In her bedroom we prepared the ventilator, piecing the various parts of the mask to the tube, breaking open the nebules of Ventolin and Atrovent and mixing them into the nebuliser.

Unscrewing. Screwing. Until all she had to do was put the mask on her face and flick the switch on the machine. She entered the times of her medication into a notebook beside her bed so she wouldn't forget. Every four or five hours. I checked. The book and a pencil were there. She preferred pencil to pen. In recent years her dependency on the machine had increased because of the deteriorating condition of her lungs, but that was to be expected, considering her age. And to think that when I came to this country I didn't even know what a headache powder was, she used to say.

At the front door I kissed her goodbye and gave her a hug, like I always did. I'll call you tomorrow, Mum. I have to go to collect some books from a publisher, but I can come around after that if you need me.

Books, books, why do you keep writing those books. Is anyone ever going to read them? Forget them … You've written enough. Give your mind a rest.

I enjoy writing, you know that … It gives me a hobby, as you've said before. And it doesn't do anyone any harm.

Drive carefully. Please forgive what I said before. I'm just a silly old woman.

No, you're not. There's nothing to forgive. You said what you needed to say, whatever the reason. That's all it was. You're my mother and I love you. No, don't come outside. It's cold. Again, I put my arms around her and hugged her, gave her a kiss. She seemed so small, with such tiny shoulders. She was like a child.

I turned around and walked away. At the front gate I stopped and waved back. She did likewise.

I got into my car and saw that she was still there, at the front door, silhouetted in the doorway, waiting for me to drive off.

I started the car, turned it around and looked back over my shoulder. She was gone.

When I arrived home I discovered she'd already telephoned to tell my family that I wasn't staying the night, that I'd left and was on my way home. She spoke to Anna. According to her, Mum sounded happy. Did I have to call back? No. Everything's fine. No need to call back. I heard a clock ticking, even though there was no clock in the room where I was standing. Then I noticed it was my wristwatch, the one she gave me in 1968, amplified in my head, sounding like a time bomb.

Next Stop for Me, Doctor ...

Thursday, 23 June 1994

After speaking at Auburn Girls' High School on *Immigrant Chronicle*, I drove over to visit Mum and Dad; it was just after twelve o'clock and I thought I might be able to have lunch with them. They weren't expecting me so it would be a surprise. The surprise, however, turned out to be mine — and in the most dramatic way.

He's been like this since Tuesday, my mother said. He's not well. Won't eat. Won't let me call the doctor. Keeps to his room. Won't talk much. He's in pain. You can tell. Look at the colour of his face.

Dad was in his room, lying on the bed, face to the wall, dressed in trousers and a singlet. I managed to get him to sit up and slowly coaxed him into talking. There was two or three days' stubble-growth on his face. His hands were cold. His skin was more blue than grey.

He described a pain that he'd felt in his right shoulder, a pain that travelled across his chest and into his left side. Everything hurts, he kept repeating. His voice sounded tired, ancient, older than his eighty-nine years. There was a remoteness in it, as if he were speaking from somewhere other than the room we were in.

We made our way into the lounge room and I insisted we call the doctor. No, no, my father said. I don't want the doctor. He started to wave his arms about, and at the same time began what I could only describe as "ramblings" — sentences that were unrelated, that seemed to just come into his mind. He seemed confused. One sentence wasn't finished before he began another, as if his memory were failing … His life in Poland, being in forced labour for five years on a farm in Germany during the Second World War, his house, his garden, Mum, myself, his grandchildren. Family names from Poland. Some I recognised; others meant nothing to me. All this "hard work" in Australia, the Water Board, "everything was coming down to this …" Coming down to what? Before he could protest further I rang for the doctor, who arrived within the hour. In the meantime, my father still refused to eat, partly withdrew into that cave of silence in which I'd found him, and sat down on the lounge opposite the front door. He insisted it be left open so he could look out on to the garden.

Dr John Hehir, an Irishman, examined my father and took me aside. Peter, this is serious. Feliks has had a coronary. He must go to hospital.

Why?

There's not much I can do here, he said.

Why, what did you hear? As he spoke, I watched the silver stethoscope reflected in the circular mirror opposite us. What can the hospital do?

The hospital can make him comfortable. He might pick up for a few days. Peter, it's called "the heart's death-rattle".

So that was it. We were talking indirectly about my father's death, right there, in his presence. It never occurred to me to object to the suggestion that he should go to hospital. I turned around, explaining to my father what the doctor thought was best to do. My mother, who would usually involve herself in something like this, remained in the background, listening. My father shook his head and stood up, catching me by surprise with the lucidity of his reply: Next stop for me, Doctor, is Rookwood. He spoke shyly, almost apologetically, as if it were wrong to question a medical man's opinion. He was pointing to the doctor, and it appeared that he was reprimanding him, but he was simply stressing the point he was making. Suddenly, the old man who had been speaking as if he couldn't string two sentences together — as if he'd become unintelligible in his thoughts — brought the whole conversation to an end in the most crystal-clear statement. All this time he'd been listening, knowing what the doctor was referring to. My mother joined in at that point and agreed it was best for him to stay at home, for the doctor and us to make him as comfortable as possible and we, the family, would look after him, see him through whatever the next couple of days brought.

Sure, the doctor agreed. He told me to stay in touch. He was going to a conference in Canberra on the weekend but would stop in on Saturday morning. He left some morphine tablets and told my mother to give him one tomorrow if the pain was still there, if ordinary painkillers were of no help.

After Dr Hehir left I reassured my mother that Dad would be alright for the next few hours and that I'd return that night to check on him. He became silent, as if he'd accepted his fate, and remained his stoic self. Maybe the doctor was wrong; maybe it wasn't what he'd diagnosed. Dad had had several turns similar to this in recent times and always managed to get through them. His resilience was of the Old Warrior kind, strong, silent, ingrained with a determination that had helped him survive those five years of forced labour in Germany; but even as we were putting him to bed he was complaining of that pain again — a pain that we thought would be helped by painkillers. His hands were cold, and, as I put him to bed and tucked his feet under the blankets, I felt the cold in them as well.

Judy accompanied me to 10 Mary Street that night. There'd been little change in Dad's condition since the afternoon. He'd eaten a little soup and bread at Mum's insistence but, once more, said he had no real appetite. The painkillers had helped somewhat, but the pain had returned and spread over his body.

He was adamant about getting fully dressed because he wanted to go to the toilet. When we suggested a dressing gown and slippers to go to the bathroom, he became distressed because we wouldn't allow him to use the outside toilet.

With the back door open, the light from the corridor and kitchen window partly illuminated the backyard as he shuffled outside, into the garden. Turn it off, he said. I know my way around without a light.

Inside the house, the three of us drank tea and talked about the day's events. What were they leading towards? Did we really suspect he was dying? I promised that I would call the doctor in the morning and report on his progress. Somewhere, out in the darkness, under clouds and starlight, my father was supposedly going to the toilet. There was no light in the outside toilet. Was he coping? Had he fallen in?

I went outside and called him, asked if he needed assistance. Go inside, he replied, I'm alright. Go inside. I'll be in soon ... Please.

His request sounded urgent, profound, yet simple. He sounded like a child who had wandered away on purpose and didn't want to be found — not an old man who had stepped out into the darkness on the night of the day his heart had had a "death-rattle".

I could make out only the outlines of fruit trees, the back fence and outside buildings. It felt spooky being out in the garden with him and not being able to see him. Cricket and frog calls floated from Duck Creek over the back fence, filling the air with the sounds of my childhood. Where exactly was he? His voice sounded like it was coming from the far end of the garden, in the left-hand corner, in what had become the last remaining vegetable patch, which he'd closed off with a fence whose stakes he'd sawed and trimmed by hand. The rest of the backyard had been turned into lawn. This had always been his sanctuary, his place of escape when he'd wanted to be alone, usually in the nearest corner, between the garage and the next-door fence. It was the garden's "blind spot", the place that couldn't be seen from the house.

By this stage it was getting late, so I returned inside. Judy said she had to go home but would return tomorrow. As she was leaving, Dad came indoors and said he was ready to go to bed. Surprised as we were, we made no remonstrative show of emotion that might make him feel as if he were being treated like an errant child. We gave him some painkillers and dressed him in his pyjamas, tucked him into bed. I told him I'd be back tomorrow. We kissed him goodnight. His body felt cold, especially the feet and hands.

Between Friday morning and Saturday night, the visits to 10 Mary Street were interrupted by other things that had to be done. Or, conversely, the routines of daily life were broken by the visits that the whole family made to 10 Mary Street.

On Friday morning Mum rang and told me she'd given him a morphine tablet. His pain was getting worse and ordinary painkillers were not helping. She had also telephoned for one of the Polish priests from Bankstown who said he would come immediately. By the time I arrived in the afternoon with Andrew and Anna, the priest had already been and gone. Mum said that Dad made his Confession and received Holy Communion. She explained that he was conscious while Father Józef Kołodziej ministered to him and he was aware of what was happening. As both parents grew older and were unable to travel to attend Mass, it was Father Józef who came weekly to 10 Mary Street and brought Holy Communion to them. We found Dad much the same as yesterday, however, although his face didn't seem to be as blue. He would start up, become agitated and then calm down. We all cried and I told both children they should think about saying their goodbyes to him. He began speaking in Polish and, again, much of what he said didn't make sense. Snippets of sentences, disjointed words; he made an effort to speak coherently, but the ability wasn't there. Or his mouth moved as if he thought he was talking but no sounds came from his throat. He requested that Andrew clip his toenails because he wanted to look good for the doctor, who, he remembered, was stopping in tomorrow. He also wanted a bath and clean pyjamas. We said we'd return and bathe him later. During the trimming of his toenails, he called Andrew "Little Peter's little boy". He began talking about his boyhood in Raciborow, Poland, and said he was running through fields of rye behind his farm. There, in those fields, he had been captured by the Nazis and marched off to forced labour in Germany. Mum, who was watching and listening, said he'd been repeating that since the morning. She told us that last night, after Judy and I left, Dad got out of bed and, in his pyjamas, returned to the garden. She gave up pleading with him to come to bed. What time he returned, she didn't know, but she thought it was around one o'clock. In the morning he was back in his bed. That struck me as being significant. Last night he didn't want to be forced to return, but wanted to be in the kitchen to say goodnight to Judy. At the same time he wanted to spend more time in his garden. Perhaps he thought he would die there? Or perhaps he came inside when he realised it was time to let go of the garden? In doing so, I later wondered, was it his way of saying goodbye to the rural life he had in Poland as well? We made our farewells, each in turn, and promised to return.

The next several hours were spent much in silence, whether we completed tasks or sat around and thought about the last twenty-four hours. Whatever the obvious was, nobody was articulating it. There was an inertia in the air, in whatever task had to be performed, that weighed down into the seconds ticking through us. You could almost hear the moments passing, feel each person's burden of thoughts. Andrew and I returned that night and bathed Dad, powdered him like a baby and put him to bed.

Mum put a woollen beanie that she'd knitted on his head and he really did look like a baby, snug in his own bed. He said, *It's warm in my bed*, and smiled. He refused food. His feet and hands were still cold. Before we left I said my good-byes to him. I held him in my arms and thanked him for look-ing after me, apologised for anything I might have done to cause him pain and told him I loved him. He nodded and we held hands. His eyes were closed. I left and Andrew said his own goodbyes.

Commitments in the city took me away until Saturday af-ternoon. When I returned, my wife and I visited Dad, and we were joined by Judy. We learnt that Dr Hehir had called in and given him another morphine tablet. Dad was sleeping when we all arrived but he woke up, startled. He still wore his beanie. I don't think he recognised me. Or any of us. Mum tried to give him some food but he brushed away her hand. She even tried to force a jelly bean into his mouth, telling him how much he liked jelly beans. He seemed to respond, to accept it, and moved his lips around as if he were sucking on it. While we sat there and talked, the jelly bean came sliding from his lips, its pink sugar-coating gone, just a little lump of gelatine remaining. I said goodbye, much the same as the day before. This time, as I held him, he didn't respond by holding my hands. His eyes were closed. There was a heaviness in his body, as if sleep had entered his body permanently.

Dad died the next morning, just before noon. I'd returned from Mass and Mum rang to say he'd stopped breathing a few minutes ago. She was by his side. I'd just got out of my car when I took the telephone call. Although it was June, it was a bright morning. The sun was on my face, birdsongs filled the garden, everything shone green with vegetation — trees, flow-ers, leaves. Jija was with me. The surroundings were similar to those Dad had chosen to be among all his life. Later, on reflec-tion, it seemed appropriate that he'd died at the outset of a new week, on a Sunday, the day that had been his traditional day of worship.

We spent most of Sunday at 10 Mary Street, saying our goodbyes to an old man who lay in his bed, small as a child, hands joined, a knitted beanie on his head, his pyjamas buttoned up under his chin, under a portrait of the Sacred Heart of Jesus and opposite a mounted poster of Pope John Paul II, the Polish Pope, a man who had been his "hero" for reasons that he never fully explained to me. Sometimes I think he admired him not because he was Christ's representative on earth, but because, through his election to the papacy, the world was shown that the Poles were not a defeated nation.

The next couple of days were spent arranging the funeral, the Requiem Mass, the grave in the family plot in the Polish section, Lawn A, in Rookwood Cemetery, that my parents had bought sixteen years earlier. Everything had been finalised except for the final inscription, the date of Dad's death — and Mum insisted that be done before the funeral. We visited a firm of stonemasons in Lidcombe to make those arrangements. Labor Funerals in Bankstown took charge of most other matters. Father Kołodziej would officiate at the Mass, to be held in the Church of St Felix de Valois, on Chapel Road in Bankstown, on Thursday, 30 June.

There was only one other formality to attend to before the funeral, and that was the private, family "viewing of the deceased" at Labor Funerals. My father would have wanted that, as he would have wished for photographs of his funeral service to be sent later to his relatives in Poland.

He lay with his hands folded, left over right, as if in prayer or contemplation, with rosary beads wound around his fingers. The liver spots on his left hand were very pronounced. I couldn't remember seeing them so dark before. Later I was to learn that this happened because the blood stops flowing in the body and rigor mortis sets in. There was a small dark spot, like a bruise, in the centre of his top lip. The crucifix of the rosary beads had been placed between his forefinger and middle finger, the way a cigarette would be held, but the placement must have looked incorrect to my mother because she adjusted it so that it lay on the top of my father's right forefinger and beneath the left. In that position, I guessed, it wouldn't fall out.

A rosewood coffin had been chosen. He lay in it dressed in his brown suit, cream-coloured shirt and brown paisley tie. The coffin's white silk lining, small pillow and lace edges somehow reminded me of christenings I'd attended, with shawls and bunny rugs in similar designs. Maybe there was a subconscious connection between the two ceremonies, one at the beginning of life, the other at the end.

The coffin lay beneath a portrait of Our Lady of Częstochowa, the Black Madonna, the Patroness of Poland. A silver crucifix stood below the portrait. Two lit candles in tall silver holders had been placed on either side of the coffin.

His hair was combed neatly, without a strand out of place. He look very rested, just like he might have been asleep, except I could only remember seeing him asleep on his side. His face was redder than his hands because of the rouge used to give his skin a more life-like complexion. When I bent down to kiss him there was a waxiness on his skin. I felt the coldness. I also noticed tiny beads of moisture, smaller than pinheads, that'd formed beneath the make-up.

We sat, we knelt, we walked around. We prayed, said the rosary, said our goodbyes over and over, talked among ourselves as if we were in our home and not that small room on South Terrace, Bankstown. Yet it was neither a room in a house nor a formal chapel. Despite its religious trappings, it was nothing more than a viewing room, but its brown decor matched the brown colours of my father's suit and that one small detail seemed to give the occasion something else, perhaps a touch of welcome, familiarity, of appropriateness.

There was no time limit to how long we could stay, but when the time came, we knew it was time to leave. I'd taken the photographs early in the visit and bade goodbye to the earthly remains of the man who had been my adopting father, my guardian, my caretaker. For some unknown reason my mind kept returning to those early years in Germany when we lived in Lebenstedt, and what I could remember of them. I wished I'd been older at the time and could have remembered more — especially the day he met my mother. Would either of them have had the slightest inkling, as they walked back in the snow after the Christmas party, that their lives would lead them to this scene opposite Bankstown railway station to-night?

That night I stayed at 10 Mary Street. For the church service my intention had been to just give the facts of my father's life, and to read the poem about him that was on the New South Wales Higher School Certificate Reading List. Instead, I wrote a eulogy that included the poem.

Next morning there were more people at St Felix's than I had expected. Many of my parents' generation had already passed away; I'd attended their funeral services in this same church. My strongest memories of the church, however, were of attending midnight Mass at Christmas many times when I was younger and the congregation singing of the Word becoming Flesh — memories of my heart and soul being filled with awe and inspiration, as these people from Poland and their descendants in Australia raised their voices in praise and thanksgiving to the God of Creation for their lives and their faith.

We sat in the front pew, on the left-hand side of the church, behind the coffin that'd been placed between us and the altar. Father Kołodziej wore a chasuble, more purple than blue, that contrasted with the red and white flowers on the coffin. I sat next to my mother.

A remoteness settled into my mind that I hadn't antici-pated, a detachment from my feelings of grief. Why wasn't I crying? That was the part that bothered me.

Later, looking at the photographs that a friend took during the Mass, there seems to be someone there who wasn't me, as I understand "me". It was almost as if I had become another person, that I wasn't Kornelia's son, or Kate's husband or the father of Judy, Andrew and Anna, all of whom sat in the pew with me. I was part of the congregation, but if I'd allowed myself to become involved in it emotionally, there and then, perhaps I wouldn't have been able to see it for the farewell to Feliks that it was, the tribute to his life and the celebration, in an external, religious sense, of his entry into Heaven.

Two moments of the service do stand out in my mind, nonetheless. The first moment was Father Kołodziej's praising my father as a good man, a hard worker, who survived the war and made a new life for himself and his family in Australia. A patriot, also, the man who never stopped loving or believing in Poland, its history and traditions; but he was also the Catholic man, the man baptised in Christ who lived that spiritual life in a practical sense by continuing to receive the sacraments all his life and never lost his faith.

The second moment was the lifting of the coffin lid so that my mother and I could say goodbye to him. It would be the last time I'd see his physical presence. His face had been covered by a square silk cloth like a handkerchief. I lifted it. His face was unchanged from the night before. Cold. Dead. At peace, whatever that meant in the world he was travelling through.

I remembered the phrase he'd used all his life whenever anybody asked him how he'd got from one place to another when there was no public transport — like the times he'd come to visit us in the camp in Parkes and there'd been no one to give him a lift from the railway station. *Na piechotę*, he'd say, "on foot". Well, Dad, I thought, you're not travelling "on foot" anymore. Wherever you are, I hope you're soaring on invisible wings, gliding, relaxing. You deserve it.

At the end of the Mass I delivered my eulogy; I reiterated some points that Father Kołodziej had made. The night before I'd got up around midnight and written down what I knew in my heart I wished to say but, until that moment, didn't quite know how to start.

I stated the facts of his life — birth, family, life on a farm, capture by the Nazis, forced labour in northern Germany for five years. His meeting with my mother in Lebenstedt Displaced Persons camp when I was three years old and their decision to emigrate to Australia. In general terms I described their life in Australia, what buying a home meant to both parents and how hard they worked to establish those front and back gardens. My father didn't believe in "sickies", I told them. The only time he had to take time off work was when he had a cancerous growth in his foot. That required an operation in Auburn District Hospital. There were two operations, in fact, because the wound refused to heal and he required a skin graft. He returned to work after his convalescence and rarely spoke about the operations. I told the congregation that he and my mother and that generation of exiles helped to make Australia what it had become. They were immigrants, part of the exodus from Europe, who arrived in the country before there were social "freebies". They made the most of the opportunities the country had to offer and took nothing for granted. I spoke of what his three grandchildren meant to him and how much he loved them. I mentioned in Polish the special terms of affection he used when they visited 10 Mary Street.

Finally, I said, in Greek mythology a hero was one who was sacrificed to Hera, wife of Zeus. Well, Dad, you made the sacrifices and survived, and that makes you a "hero" in a different sense of the word. I salute you and am proud to have your name.

To finish, I read the poem I wrote on 19 October 1971.

Feliks Skrzynecki

My gentle father
kept pace only with the Joneses
of his own mind's making —
loved his garden like an only child,
spent years walking its perimeter
from sunrise to sleep.
Alert, brisk and silent,
he swept its paths
ten times around the world.

Hands darkened
from cement, fingers with cracks
like the sods he broke,
I often wondered how he existed
on five or six hours' sleep each night —
why his arms didn't fall off
from the soil he turned
and tobacco he rolled.

His Polish friends
always shook hands too violently
I thought ... Feliks Skrzynecki,
that formal address
I never got used to.
Talking, they reminisced
about farms where paddocks flowered
with corn and wheat,
horses they bred, pigs
they were skilled in slaughtering.
Five years of forced labour in Germany
did not dull the softness of his blue eyes.

I never once heard him
complain of work, the weather

or pain. When twice
they dug cancer out of his foot,
his comment was, "but I'm alive."
Growing older, I
remember words he taught me,
remnants of a language
I inherited unknowingly —
the curse that damned
a crew-cut, grey-haired
Department clerk
who asked me in dancing-bear grunts,
"Did your father ever attempt to learn English?"

On the back steps of his house,
bordered by golden cypress,
lawns — geraniums younger
than both parents,
my father sits out the evening
with his dog, smoking,
watching stars and street lights come on,
content as I have never been.

At thirteen,
stumbling over tenses in Caesar's Gallic War,
I forgot my first Polish word.
He repeated it so I never forgot.
After that, like a dumb prophet,
watched me pegging my tents
further and further south of Hadrian's Wall.

In 1978 my parents purchased a family plot in the old Polish
Section in Rookwood Cemetery. On a slope facing the west,
below a line of brushbox trees, over the two plots, suitable for
taking four coffins, a black marble headstone was erected with
my parents' names and birthdates cut and painted in gold.

When we visited the stonemason after Dad's death, Mum arranged to have the date of Dad's death added and an enamelled photograph fixed to the centre of the headstone. Both parents had chosen their photographs when the plot was purchased — both selected their passport photographs. At first I thought this was a strange choice. Dad was eighty-nine when he died, and in the photograph he's in his mid-forties. Mum is in her early thirties in her photograph. I wondered how old she'd be when she died.

But in the visits I've made to this section of the cemetery, I've noticed over the years that there are many such enamelled photographs. Poles who were in their sixties, seventies and eighties when they died, yet with photographs on their headstones from their passports or taken decades earlier.

When I travelled to Poland in 1989 I visited the graves of my father's parents in the cemetery in Raciborow. It was never requested of me, but I returned with a handful of soil that I knew I would sprinkle on my father's coffin on the day of his funeral. Thick, heavy, black, almost like sand, the soil was kept in a sealed plastic bag. My father never once asked me its purpose, but, in the intervening years, I would occasionally take out the bag and see how the black grains were turning into grey dust.

When we arrived at the cemetery the grave had been prepared. The pallbearers carried the coffin from the hearse and laid it across the green coverlet. The rosewood coffin looked magnificent in the sunlight, shining the colour of lacquered blood. The floral tribute on top shone even brighter.

A decade of the rosary was said. A hymn was sung in Polish and the coffin blessed with holy water. Father Kołodziej performed the ceremony with dignity, with the utmost respect and care. I could not fault anything he did. I remember thinking, How many times has he done this? Yet it was like he was performing it for the first time.

The coffin was lowered, the ropes withdrawn, and it was

time for the family and myself to sprinkle the soil from Poland. Father announced this and boy, oh boy, you should have seen the stampede towards me. One man, Mr Pilsudski, rushed forward like a long-legged spider so quickly, hand held out, that he almost tripped and fell into the grave. Others followed him, mostly men. *Polska ziemia!* they repeated. "Polish soil". I asked them to stand back so that my mother and I, and my children, could sprinkle it first. It was like they were rushing forward to be fed. When the Polish soil had all been sprinkled, many still dipped their fingers into the empty plastic bag — as if the air itself was sacred. The mourners then dropped a small lump of soil or clay onto the coffin to symbolise our union with the deceased and acknowledging that we, too, one day, would follow him. Some people dropped flowers.

I stayed at Mum's the next two nights and drove her to the cemetery where she "tidied up" the grave, as she put it. For her that meant crying, praying, standing there and talking to Dad as if he were alive and in good health. It meant cleaning spots of dirt and water that'd splashed on to the marble; she'd brought along Ajax cleaner, a bucket, brush and several cleaning cloths. It also meant rearranging the flowers in the vases and the floral tributes, already soaked in moisture and decomposing in their cellophane wrappers. For me, it meant standing there and listening to everything she said to him about their life.

On Sunday night I returned home. Whatever "normal" meant, life was returning to its old pace and routines. Work. Supervising examinations. Departmental meetings. Shopping at Franklins. Spreading topsoil on the back lawn. Taking the car to Tony Garnett's West City Holden for servicing. Going to Mass. Visiting Mum … And sleep. Lots of it. As much as I could get.

Monday, 18 July 1994

Midnight

I'm in Room 33 of the Murwillumbah Motor Inn. Unable to sleep, I've been writing poetry about my father. Later today I'll be teaching Year 12 at St Patrick's College, a local Catholic high school. I've been invited to fly up to northern New South Wales and speak on *Immigrant Chronicle*.

I actually arrived on the Saturday night; because this is familiar territory to me, I decided to come before the Monday and have a whole day to myself.

It was here, in 1968, on the south arm of the Tweed River, that I received my second teaching posting, to a small school in a little village called Kunghur, half an hour's drive out of town.

When I made the booking I specifically asked for a room with a view of Mount Warning, the outstanding geographic monument that dominates the Tweed Valley. When I taught here, its presence — physically, mentally, spiritually — would occupy my thoughts for hours on end ... Hours. Days. Weeks. Months. Its peak is the first part of Australia to be touched by the rays of the rising sun. It figures in Aboriginal mythology, and there are many legends associated with its creation. It is supposed to be the central link in Australia's mandala of stones.

On Sunday I went to Mass and spent the greater part of the morning walking around Murwillumbah, taking photographs, revisiting old shopping streets and walking along the Tweed River where it flows alongside the Pacific Highway.

Lush green vegetation.

Sugar cane plantations.

Banana plantations.

The old bridge standing beside the new bridge, near the railway station, along the road that brings the visitor into town.

Giant palm trees growing along the river.

Blue. Green. Blue. Green.

I can feel the energy of light.

Smell the vegetation.

Hear roots growing in the earth.

How many times did the locals tell me back in 1968 that this was "God's own country"?

But as I was writing the poetry, I looked back on the day and I knew that the walk I took was not just a stroll through yesterday's shadows. Something had been happening inside me; I can't say exactly when it entered my blood, but a terrible longing, *żal*, was building up in me, pulling me slowly but surely back to my father's death. I began to miss him like I hadn't missed him in the three weeks since he'd died. My body was hit with spasms as I walked, like I was having stomach cramps. I would sob, but the tears just wouldn't break. It lasted most of the day, even when I took myself to the Regent in the afternoon to see *Farewell My Concubine* ... But it was there, in the darkness, that the first tears came, hot and fast, not loud and bawling, but soft. A weeping. A steady continuous weeping.

Why couldn't I have cried like that in the church of St Felix de Valois in Bankstown, when I sat like a ghost, almost like I wasn't there? Or by the graveside, surrounded by family and friends? Or at Mum's? Why did it have to be here, in a movie theatre only half full, so far from home, among strangers?

As I wrote, the shape of Mount Warning loomed over the horizon like an ancient deity that I could see in my mind's eye — the same shape that followed me everywhere I went in 1968, at whose foothills my small school nestled like a red-capped bird. All the time watching. Watching. Saying nothing. But watching. Speaking to me like an older brother or sister might. Or a parent. Or a teacher. Or God. And the longing for my father, his presence, there, all the time, drawing me towards something dark and strong, a long wide river, perhaps, something I knew I'd never understand, but ultimately that didn't matter, because I'd already accepted it and written the poem that'd helped me as I floundered through the darkness and then out of it.

Alone in Murwillumbah

The effect you had on me was the effect
you could not help having.
> — Franz Kafka, *Letter to His Father*

Going to Mass
at the Church of the Sacred Heart,
I pray for my father
who died three weeks ago today —
so far from here, but still
in my heart: the Polish immigrant
who lies buried under
dying flowers in Rookwood's graveyard.

Revisiting the old haunts
of twenty-six years ago
where I taught in this green valley
and daily became homesick
like a lost child —
I take photos of Mount Warning,
the Tweed River
and various streets: as if to remind
myself later, in Sydney, that I was actually here.

To fill the hours
of late afternoon, I go
to the Regent and see
Farewell My Concubine —
drawn by what I remember
as being favourable reviews.

Something inside me reacts
to the violence, to scenes
of death and pain —
something I can't put my finger on
but find myself weeping for
in the dark: grateful
for the peace my father
had brought into my life.

Walking home
the old contours
of roads and hills return —
familiar though grown smaller:
Riverview Street,
Wollumbin, Byangum Road.

Darkness blots out
the shape of Mount Warning
from which I've always got my bearings.
"It's all right, Dad," I whisper.
"Stay with me.
I know exactly where I'm going."

Closed Venetian Blinds

Thursday, 6 February 1997

The sun's intensity is apparent even before it begins its morning climb. It's supposed to be the end of summer but it's just as bad as over Christmas and during January. Hot. Sticky and hot. Try to get the day's chores over by lunchtime and then stay indoors with the airconditioner turned on.

In the morning, driving over to Hale and Iremonger, I kept reliving last night at Mum's.

Again I could feel the strange atmosphere in the house, the almost static breathing of the house, as if everything in it was paused on the brink of an abyss, holding its breath, waiting for something to happen. There was no tension. All apprehensions were gone. The hard words, the anger, the stress and trials of past years were gone. I remembered when, a few months earlier, I'd asked her to tell me my biological father's name and she did. She also drew my attention to a small photograph in the box where she'd kept my First Holy Communion medal and other souvenirs. The photograph is of three men. He's the one in front, she said.

But it was just my mother and myself, watching a black-and-white movie about an old man's achievements and memories. We were having a cup of tea, watching images on a TV screen, listening to words and the silences between them. Then her sudden dismissal of me, her abstract statement in Polish, "No, what will be will be." My farewell to her. The kiss. The hug. Telling her that I loved her. The promise to ring today.

But when I returned from Alexandria and rang, she didn't answer the telephone. I went shopping. Andrew had gone fishing. Judy came over to get her camera checked out at the local camera shop where she'd bought it because it wasn't winding. After she went, I tried ringing Mum again. No answer. I decided to drive over. Surely if she hadn't been feeling well she would have rung me?

After Dad died we had an agreement that as soon as she woke up each morning she'd open her Venetian blinds. This way, even if I was running late for work and didn't have time to stop in, at least I knew she was all right.

In retrospect, it was the steadiest, calmest drive in my life. Almost as if the car was driving itself. Or, inexplicably, as if a power beyond myself and the car had taken over. Was in control.

I pulled up outside 10 Mary Street and the blinds were closed. Did I know unconsciously what I would find? Again, in retrospect, I think that I did. Yet, from the time I closed the car door to the time I reached the back of the house, I argued with myself that there was an explanation other than what I was dreading.

The back door was closed from the inside and the key was in the door — which meant I couldn't use my key to get in. Standing on a garden bench and using a screwdriver that I found in the laundry, I was able to force a back window and climb in.

The house was in absolute stillness. It was stuffy, hot. It'd been closed up all day.

The only sounds were my breathing and my beating heart.

Standing in the kitchen, I called out, but there was no reply. I ran to Mum's bedroom but couldn't see her. I could now hear another sound — a mechanical, humming sound. Where was she? Where?

She wasn't in the bathroom, nor in Dad's room. I ran outside, calling her. No reply.

Back in the house, I retraced my steps.

From room to room. Nothing.

Except that humming sound coming from her room.

I ran inside, this time to the far side of the bed.

What tore from inside me was a cry, a scream, a howl of protest, pain, disbelief. It was all those things and yet it was something beyond them all. Months later I remember thinking how eerie the cry sounded — it was like I was being murdered.

My mother lay on the floor, on her right side, almost in a foetal position, her head in a pool of blood. The ventilator mask was on her face and the humming sound was coming from the ventilator on the fold-up dinner tray she used by the side of her bed. The biggest shock came when I saw that the right side of her face looked like it had been smashed in with a shovel. I removed the mask and saw that it was swollen grossly, to the point of disfigurement, more black than blue and purple, caked with blood. When I lifted her head, fresh blood ran from her ear. I tried to lift her, pull her up on to the bed but couldn't. She was cold.

Immediately I rang Dr Hehir and told him Mum was dead. What! he cried out. I'll be straight over.

I rang home and told my wife to let the rest of the family know. I also rang Kevin Coates, my mate from St Patrick's.

I turned off the ventilator and noticed for the first time that the bed light was turned on. She kept a notebook beside the bed, and after using the ventilator she would write down the time. This was every four or five hours. The last entry read "ten to twelve". It was now just after four o'clock. My mother had been dead for approximately sixteen hours.

The doctor confirmed what I'd worked out myself before anyone else arrived. Mum must have got up to use the ventilator and died of cardiac arrest while on the machine. She had slipped off the side of the bed and hit her head on the floor.

The blood, all from her right ear, had congealed on the side of her face and also soaked into the carpet and bedclothes.

When the doctor arrived and we lifted her on to the bed, the blood ran freely for a short time and stopped.

Peter, the doctor said, she was dead before she hit the floor. She felt no pain. She would have closed her eyes and felt as if she was going to sleep.

The family arrived, one by one, as did Kevin, and we said our goodbyes to her. The doctor wrote out the death certificate. I rang Labor Funerals in Bankstown.

Left alone with her, I don't know at what point I stopped crying, or, indeed, if I did. She seemed so small, so vulnerable. She'd told me more than once she didn't want to be buried with her golden earrings, so I removed them. That she was dead, that she was so badly bruised, that she was bloodied and cold made no difference. She was still my mother. I held her and whispered that I loved her.

Mum's funeral took place the following Tuesday, 11 February. As with Dad's funeral, Requiem Mass was in St Felix de Valois Catholic Church, Bankstown, and Father Kołodziej officiated.

She was buried with Dad in the family plot, Grave 973, Lawn A.

This time there was no soil from Poland to sprinkle on to the coffin.

As we were leaving it began to rain.

I was surprised to see how many of her friends turned up at the reception afterwards at 10 Mary Street, people that I'd forgotten from the early days in the migrant camps and from various western suburbs in Sydney. Mr and Mrs Budzinski from Yagoona. Children of Doctor and Mrs O'Brien of Strathfield, whom she'd worked for in the 1950s and early 1960s, were there, as were Mr Laurie O'Neil, his wife Philomena and their son Michael. My former English teacher from St Patrick's, Brian Couch, under whom I'd studied English Honours, surprised me with his presence, as did Brothers Brian Berg and Julian McDonald. Colleagues of mine from work, and old school friends and their wives, all came to say their farewells and lend support.

When I shook the tablecloths on to the back lawns, in a light rain, sparrows flew out from among the salvias — as if they'd been waiting for the crumbs.

By three o'clock all the guests had left. The house was closed up but I knew I'd return tomorrow.

Going home, I detoured via the cemetery because I wanted to get some more photographs. By now the rain was starting and stopping frequently and more was predicted for the rest of the week. I couldn't help but smile at one of my mother's sayings, "The one who sends the rain will also send the sun." The rain held off while I took the photographs.

Sayings

While she was alive
I took my mother's sayings for granted —
those lines of words that came
so easily into her head
as if she were turning on a tap:

"Go slowly and you'll go further."
"Buy not buy but try."
"Having one child is like having
one eye in your head."
Or, "I'm not from the stepmother."

Sometimes they made sense;
mostly they didn't — not that I bothered
to stop and ask questions,
to think about anything that ran
deeper in my heart than blood.

Now that she's dead they all make sense —
short, humorous, elliptical,
like blows to the head or heart:
spot on, up close, hard,
never missing their mark.

Sprzedaj!

Today I spent several hours at 10 Mary Street. While the sprinklers watered the garden I aired the house, opened every door and window and marked students' assignments I'd brought over with me.

Strange how everything here has aged all of a sudden. There's a tenuous feeling in the air, a quiet, thin strain as if something's about to break — something I won't want to know about when it does, even though this day was perhaps the best time I've had here, alone, since late autumn. The house needed the visit. I needed the visit.

In church this morning I'd listened to a sermon about suffering, about acceptance of everything that we are born to. Nothing will ever change these Absolutes, and all the fret and worry in the world won't relieve our anguish.

The quotation the priest used and later I found in the Bible cryptically accorded our days their importance:

As for man, his days are as grass:
As a flower of the field so he flourisheth.
For the wind passeth over it, and it is gone;
And the place thereof shall know it no more.

King David was right. We are like weeds.

My father weeded these lawns diligently by hand and now he's dead. Weeds grow across the lawns and the flowers will start dying unless I keep coming back to water them. Where are the vegetables that grew so abundantly in the backyard?

As I was leaving across the front lawn, the lawn squelching under my shoes, the house said, Thanks.

Thanks for everything, I replied.

Getting into my car, the words of a Creedence Clearwater Revival song came into my head, *There's a bad moon on the rise ...*

The first noticeable thing about the sign that's been put up in the front garden of 10 Mary Street is the word AUCTION, in big white letters against a red background.

The second thing that strikes me is the catch-phrase, one of those seductive clichés that estate agents use with flair, as if they'd invented the English language, BACKS ONTO RESERVE. Hopefully, this will be one of the property's strengths, one of its selling points.

In smaller lettering, the sign says, 3 BEDROOMS, NEAT AND READY TO LIVE IN.

There is a contact name and mobile telephone number, as well as the address of Nolan's First National in Burwood.

I've chosen a mate, Matt Nolan, from St Patrick's College, Strathfield, to sell 10 Mary Street. The date for the auction will be Saturday, 16 August, at 2 p.m. Matt's name stands out almost as prominently as the telephone number below "Nolan's First National Real Estate". Notices for the sale have been put into the *Sydney Morning Herald* and the local newspapers in the inner-city suburbs where Matt's business is located. This will continue for a month. This way, he believes, it will attract not just buyers but also property investors.

The sale is the culmination of months of deliberation as to whether or not I should sell the house. The issue had been going around in my head like a spinning top. Finally, when the decision was made to sell, it came through a set of circumstances so dramatic and unforeseen that no one in my family or in the circle of friends closest to me could have predicted them, not in their wildest dreams or guesses.

The colours of the sign are red, blue and white. I look at them and unconsciously make associations with the Union Jack, with royalty, with the rhyme I learnt in the playground at St Peter Chanel's:

Red, white and blue,
the girls love you —
they kiss you at the pictures
and hug you at the zoo.

Blue symbolises spatial distances, sky and sea. Red, as on the Polish flag, stands for death, blood and sacrifice. White, also on the flag, for purity and redemption, the Resurrection. As remote as it is, as highly improbable, I like to think that these three colours, in combination, in front of the house that was my home, is not just coincidental, that perhaps there is Providence in their presence, like a sign of hope.

As I take a photograph of the house in the morning light, it reflects the rising sun off its tiles and brickwork. Shadows fall across the fence from the two brushbox trees growing on the nature strip, one in front of our home and one from next door, Number 8. When the sun rises higher and the shadows lengthen they will merge, creating one large shadow over the house that is pleasant to have in summer because it makes the house cool in the mornings.

The roses have been pruned but the brunfelsias are in bloom.

The leaves on the gardenias are a yellow-green.

Even though it's winter and the grass doesn't grow much, it's been cut and the edges trimmed.

The gates are closed and the yard is spotless.

Strangely, I don't feel any regret in agreeing to sell the house after the shock of what happened.

When I drove away from Parkes the morning after my interview with Peter Tom was finished, I expected to be drawn back to a last look at the site of the migrant camp. The foundations and concrete blocks that were there when I first returned in 1984 had been removed. Tall grasses waved in the breeze. The trees growing along the side of the road had concealed the site that'd now become another lot of paddocks on a farmer's property. But the last look didn't eventuate. There was no slowing down or pulling over to the side of the road. I just kept driving into the morning sun, towards Orange, the Blue Mountains and home.

So too, here, I don't deviate from the decision I made or, rather, the decision made for me by the person least expected and yet the one person whom I should have known would make it for me during the preceding months of deliberation.

What happened couldn't have been avoided, either physically or mentally, even if I'd run to the end of the street or attempted to jump into outer space to try and escape the experience.

She was there, waiting, like she always waited when I needed help, whether it was after being pulled out of a cesspool or when I was too afraid to tell the nuns I wouldn't be going on any more errands for them because I'd caught a cold the last time they sent me to the butcher's in the rain. Like she said she'd be there the morning the two zebra finches flew into the yard.

It was time to let go of the house, unequivocally, and so, shortly after 28 June, everything was prepared for the sale. Like the sign on the front lawn said, the house was NEAT AND READY TO LIVE IN.

On Thursday, 26 June 1997, my wife was diagnosed with leukaemia.

We entered the doctor's surgery at 7 p.m. that night. As soon as the door was closed and we sat down, he said, Kate, I'm not going to beat about the bush. You've got leukaemia.

No sooner had he finished those words, at that precise moment, I knew that our lives would never be the same again.

We discussed how she hadn't been feeling well that week, the results of the blood tests she'd had done, how abnormally high her white cell count was and the type of leukaemia she'd been diagnosed with. We were told she'd have to start chemotherapy the very next day. The situation was "life-threatening".

Shock. Disbelief. Bewilderment. Why?

The next two days were the kind of nightmare you read about or hear about or watch in a movie. Your life becomes a series of events that happen to other people. You never think they might touch your life. Or, if you do think about them, you push them out of your mind quickly because their details become too painful.

Journal notes help me keep track of each day.

Friday, 27 June 1997

We go to the San (Adventist Hospital). K's haematologist is Dr Margot Harris. Tests and treatment begin straightaway. I stay till 3 p.m ... Others visit, relatives, friends. In the evening I return ... I feel like being angry, crying, everything, all emotions all at once ... K doesn't deserve this ... I can't get over the shock. She's being so brave about it, positive, has a really healthy attitude to it all ...

It rains lightly that evening, though in the morning I will doubt the heaviness of rain when I discover another kind of damage and find footsteps where I don't expect to find footsteps.

Saturday, 28 June 1997

I have to go to work in the morning to attend to a few matters that it wasn't possible to get done yesterday.

On the way over I stop to check on 10 Mary Street.

As I walk down the side of the house I notice that the flyscreens from the two windows are lying on the ground. How could that be? It rained last night, but — how — how could rain remove flyscreens? Was it a heavy wind? A storm? I don't remember a storm warning for any part of Sydney on the weather report! It wasn't raining that heavily on the drive home from the hospital. But then, winds don't undo flyscreens and remove them!

As I turn the corner of the house I see that the flyscreens from the back windows are also on the ground. The window in the small bedroom, the "spare room", as it was called, has been smashed!

It happens just like that — an instantaneous realisation that there's been a break-in and the sound of my mother's voice, sharp, clear, *Sprzedaj!* The word means "sell", and all of a sudden the deliberation, the dilly-dallying over what to do with the house is over!

Later, in the months and years after the new owners have moved in, I ponder over that experience. I know what I heard and I know how I heard it. It wasn't just with my ears but with every part of me. It seemed that I first heard it in my gut and then it moved like a flash of light, spontaneously, outwards, into every part of me. My mother didn't sound angry, but she sounded strict. It wasn't just a request. It was an order. Do it!

I manage to crawl in through the smashed window and find blood on the carpet in the room and in the kitchen. Going through the house, I find chairs and lamps tipped over, drawers in the sideboard pulled open and rifled. The small bedside cabinet in Dad's bedroom is turned over and its contents scattered — so too the dressing table drawers. The wardrobe doors have been left flung open.

In the hallway the linen press has had its contents dragged out, sheets, pillowcases, the leather bag containing my parents' letters from Europe over the years and many of the birthday and Christmas cards they received.

In the main bedroom the top of my mother's sewing machine has been opened and the machine is missing. The two wardrobes have had their contents searched and my mother's old black leather handbag, the one she stopped using years ago, pulled out. In it, she kept a collection of fifty-cent pieces. It's gone. Probably fifty or sixty dollars. She kept those coins for good luck. The only luck to come from this break-and-enter is — as the police will tell me when I report the crime — the fact that the thief didn't trash the place.

When the police arrive we search the yard and house and find fresh footprints in the garden behind the garage. They trail through the garden plots, going west. The police officers deduce that the thief got out of the yard by climbing over the fence. After I ring a glass company to come and fix the window, I ring Andrew and ask him to stay at 10 Mary Street while I go to work.

That evening I visit Kate in hospital. She is in a buoyant mood. She feels more positive than yesterday that she will beat this illness. I return to 10 Mary Street and stay the night.

Sunday, 29 June 1997

Early in morning to home and hospital. It's going to be a long year. Dr Harris tells me that "the penny hasn't dropped for your wife. She doesn't have any idea what she's in for. It'll get a lot worse"... I want to sleep. Andrew stayed overnight at Mum's ... Until it's sold the house will need watching ...

The house failed to sell at auction.

Only a small number of people turned up and no one bid. Judy accompanied me. To my surprise, Tony Garnett, who was also a school friend from St Patrick's College, arrived to lend his support.

The trips to and from the hospital because of Kate's illness had become a regular part of our lives, had assumed a priority above all else. The children helped out and provided transport, as did friends, when I wasn't able to because of work. Words and phrases like "stem cells", "biopsy", "chemotherapy", "acute myloid leukaemia", "bone marrow" and "transplant" were now part of our daily conversations.

After a meeting with Matt Nolan I decided to advertise the sale of 10 Mary Street in the local newspaper, the one serving the Lidcombe, Berala, Regents Park and Sefton areas. I said if he wouldn't do it, then I'd do it myself. He agreed to.

The response was immediate. In one afternoon alone, four couples inspected the house and two made offers.

On 4 September I accepted the offer made by a Pakistani family. Contracts were exchanged on Friday, 19 September.

Five weeks later the removalists arrived to empty the contents of the house. The majority of the furniture was going into storage, some of it to Judy's unit. A few weeks earlier, Andrew and I had borrowed a truck from West City Holden and spent the day transporting belongings from 10 Mary Street to my home — garden furniture, pot plants, most of the contents of the garage, whatever held sentimental value, like the "wooden horse" that my father built and used for carpentry, or the old yellow Pope hand-mower that my father preferred to use even after he'd bought a petrol mower.

In those weeks, on two or three occasions, I met the new owners of the house, husband, wife, daughter, three sons — warm, friendly people who came to have a close inspection of the house and even brought me a meal. One day, when I had a camera with me, I took their photographs in the front garden, in the same spot where Mum and Dad and I had ours taken nearly fifty years earlier. I promised them I'd get the photographs to them when the film was developed. As I was showing them the backyard, the second-eldest son asked me what was in the chookshed. I explained that there was nothing in there now but perches, empty nest boxes and, in the corner, a cage where we once bred chicks and ducklings. When he saw it he jumped up, calling out to his father, Can we have rabbits there, please? Can we have rabbits? His father laughed and said, yes, he'd let them have rabbits. The boy ran out into the yard, joining his brothers and sister, calling, Hooray, hooray, we're going to have rabbits!

Something inexplicable drew me back to 10 Mary Street twenty-four hours before settlement. Kate had been allowed to come home for the night from RPA where she was now being treated in preparation for her bone-marrow transplant. Professor John Gibson was now in charge. At about nine o'clock at night I drove over. What did I expect to find? Another break-in? Revellers on the lawns? Ghosts on the roof?

I expected nothing and found nothing — nothing except a house in darkness, breathing, asleep. Was it dreaming?

Because of a technical delay between solicitors, settlement of the house was held over until Thursday, 30 October — the same day as Kate was having her transplant. It had been discovered that her brother, John, was a perfect bone-marrow match and that, we believed, augured well for a recovery.

Payment for the house, however, could not be made for another six days. When it was, I received it from my solicitor and next day drove over to Nolan's First National and handed over the keys.

On Friday, 7 November, I returned to 10 Mary Street for the last time, intending to give copies of the photographs to the new family. It was after work and late, towards dusk, but the family was not alone, it seemed. The front veranda was full of furniture. There were several cars parked outside and the house was full of voices. Lights were on in all the rooms. I put the photographs into the letterbox. No *żal*. Only the sparrows in the garden, in the brushbox trees on the nature strip, settling down for the night. I remembered the dreams I'd had of both parents since they died; sometimes they were in the same spot where I stood now. They always looked younger than when they died and seemed to be moving on to somewhere else. Maybe that was their message to me? Let go of the past. Move on.

As I drove away I saw two old people side by side in the garden, a man and a woman, stooped among the roses that had come into bloom, in the shadows, looking up at the departing figure getting into his car and driving off. He didn't look back, but if he had, a few moments later, he would have seen that they, too, were gone. In their place, children were running out of the house, into the garden, laughing and playing, calling out, Hooray, hooray! We're going to have rabbits! Hooray!

Only Child

For as long as he can remember
he was always good with words —
the little boy who stared through the window
and listened to how the wind made the grass sing.
He would wait alone in a room
for his mother to come home from work —
from a place "out there", whatever
that meant, while the clock's hands moved
so very very slowly until the door opened
and she stood there, smiling, arms held out to him.

It was during those times of being alone
that he managed to put sounds together —
somehow welded a feeling in his blood
with the sounds it would create in his head.
Cold when he shivered and had no coat.
Warm when he snuggled under the eiderdown.
Go away when he was angry with someone.
Please stay when he was frightened
of being left alone in the room.

His childhood had become a series
of arrivals and departures, packed suitcases
left waiting at the front door
for a bus or truck to transport him
and his mother to the next Displaced Persons' camp.
"One day it will change," his mother told him.
"One day we will settle down in a house of our own —
Have a garden, grow vegetables and flowers.
You can have your own puppy. One day
You will understand what our lives were about."

Now his mother is dead and his adopting father.
His own life has passed the fifty-year mark.
Often he prefers the company of music and books
to the presence of other human beings.
He trusts very few people apart from his own family
and could spend all day watching the flights of birds
if time and circumstances permitted the luxury.

Words come easily, almost indifferently,
but he says nothing and sinks into his own well of silence —
in whose depths he hears the same kind of music
he heard when left alone as a child
and the wind scattered its treasure of vowels and consonants
for him to discover in the long grass.